SALVAGE

Basic Theory of
Lasers and Masers

Documents on Modern Physics

Edited by

ELLIOT W. MONTROLL, *University of Rochester*
GEORGE H. VINEYARD, *Brookhaven National Laboratory*
MAURICE LÉVY, *Université de Paris*
P. T. MATTHEWS, *Imperial College, London University*

Basic Theory of
Lasers and Masers

A Density Matrix Approach

JACQUES VANIER

Université Laval, Québec, Canada

GORDON AND BREACH SCIENCE PUBLISHERS

New York   London   Paris

To Lucie, Lyne, and Pierre

Preface

THE DENSITY MATRIX formalism is one of the most useful tools for solving problems encountered in the study of ensembles of identical particles which cooperate to a given phenomenon. The formalism is most useful in magnetic resonance and quantum electronics; this is specially true when one deals with problems encountered in the fields of masers and lasers. It is true that all the information that is obtained is already contained in Schrödinger and Heisenberg representations of quantum mechanics. However the formalism makes it possible to obtain the information much more easily. This is due to the fact that the particles are considered as a single ensemble, which is described by one unique matrix called the density matrix. When that matrix is known all the information on the ensemble can be obtained.

The present monograph describes in some detail the density matrix formalism and gives the methods for using it in connection with problems of quantum electronics. In order to study the subject, the reader does not need an advanced quantum mechanics course. Only basic principles are needed and those are given in the first chapter. Emphasis is put somewhat on the concept of angular momentum since it plays a major role in the following chapters.

I would like to thank all those who have contributed to the realisation of the present monograph specially the group of the Quantum Electronics Laboratory who have helped much by their constructive criticism. I would like also to thank Prof. G. A. Woonton who has been a guide for me during my first years of acquaintance with the subject.

The present book owes a considerable debt to texts like *Principles of Magnetic Resonance* by C. P. Slichter and the *Principles of Nuclear Magnetism* by A. Abragam.

J. VANIER

ix

Contents

CHAPTER 1

Introductory Quantum Mechanics

IN THE PRESENT chapter, the concepts basic to the theory of quantum mechanics are stated. No attempt is made to develop or prove those concepts in a formal way. Only under certain circumstances is a mathematical derivation given, for example, in those places which are not covered specifically in standard textbooks. Furthermore, only the concepts essential to the understanding of the chapters which follow are given.

For a more formal treatment the reader is referred to any standard textbook on quantum mechanics; references to several of these are given in the bibliography at the end of this monograph.

1.1 THE BASIC POSTULATES

Quantum mechanics can be developed from a few basic principles. These principles give the rules that govern the microscopic world of atomic structures. They can be expressed in various forms. The key to the whole theory, however, is contained in Schrödinger's equation which states that the wave function Ψ which describes the behaviour of an atomic particle varies with time according to the equation:

$$\mathcal{H}_{op}\Psi = i\hbar \frac{\partial}{\partial t}\Psi \qquad (1.1)$$

where $\mathcal{H}_{op}$ is the hamiltonian describing the interaction of the particle with its surrounding. In quantum mechanics, $\mathcal{H}$, the hamiltonian, is treated as an operator which operates on the wave function Ψ. The rules by which the classical hamiltonian, which is effectively the total energy of the system, is put into an operator form, are given by the so-called Schrödinger representation. These rules form part of the basic postulates.

A BASIC POSTULATE   To every dynamical variable (or observable) of classical mechanics, there corresponds an operator; the correspondence can be given as follows:

Variable in classical representation	Quantum mechanical representation
position xyz or other set of coordinates	x, y, z, which means when operating on a function, multiply from the left
Momentum $p_x = mv_x$ and similarly for other coordinates	$-i\hbar \dfrac{\partial}{\partial x}$ and similar expressions for other coordinates
Total energy E	$+i\hbar \dfrac{\partial}{\partial t}$
Potential energy V	V

These operators operate on the wave function Ψ called the operand. According to these rules, the classical expression for the hamiltonian $\mathscr{H}$

$$\mathscr{H} = \frac{1}{2m} p^2 + V = \text{total energy } E \tag{1.2}$$

is readily transformed to

$$\left(-\frac{\hbar^2}{2m} \nabla^2 + V \right)\Psi = -i\hbar \frac{\partial \Psi}{\partial t} \tag{1.3}$$

Special attention is paid to the behaviour of Ψ. According to accepted practice $\Psi^*\Psi$ is referred as the probability density and $\Psi^*\Psi\, d\tau$ is the probability of finding the particle in the volume element $d\tau$.

A SECOND POSTULATE   The wave function and its first derivative with respect to coordinate must be continuous, finite and single valued over all space. It also follows that since $\Psi^*\Psi$ is the probability density, there should be a certainty of finding the particle somewhere; consequently we must have;

$$\int \Psi^*\Psi\, d\tau = 1 \tag{1.4}$$

The statement of the correspondence between quantum mechanical operators and classical dynamical variables does not mention anything about the possible values of a measurement of the variables; another postulate fills this need.

A THIRD POSTULATE   The expectation value $\langle Q \rangle$ of an observable, represented in quantum mechanics by an operator Q_{op}, is given by the relation

$$\langle Q \rangle = \int\limits_{-\infty}^{+\infty} \Psi^* Q_{op} \Psi\, d\tau \tag{1.5}$$

This is the mean value that is expected from many measurements made on the observable Q. The expression above is written in a symbolic form as

$$\langle Q \rangle = \langle \Psi \, | Q_{op} | \, \Psi \rangle \tag{1.6}$$

where Dirac notation of bra. $\langle \Psi |$ and ket. $| \Psi \rangle$ is used and $\langle Q \rangle$ is the value that would be obtained from a measurement on the observable represented by Q_{op}. If $\langle Q \rangle$ is effectively the eigenvalue of Q_{op} then Ψ is an eigenfunction of Q_{op}.

In most cases with which we will be concerned, the hamiltonian will take the form of the interaction of a magnetic moment, with a magnetic field. This interaction is then simply:

$$\mathcal{H} = \boldsymbol{\mu} \, . \, \mathbf{H} \tag{1.7}$$

where H is a magnetic field which may be time dependent and $\boldsymbol{\mu}$ is the magnetic moment which has to be represented by an operator. This operator is normally directly proportional to the angular momentum operator. We shall describe this last one in a later section. Our problem thus consists in solving equation (1.1). Solving it for one particle is already a complex problem and for more complicated systems, only approximate solutions can be obtained. It is here that the tools of statistical mechanics, such as the formalism of the density matrix, becomes extremely useful. Nothing new is introduced that is not already in equation (1.1), our starting point, but it does simplify the mathematics of treating the problems of an ensemble of N similar bodies that may interact with each others as well as with external fields.

1.2 FORMAL SOLUTION OF SCHRÖDINGER'S EQUATION

In the case, $\mathcal{H}_{op}$ is independent of time, equation (1.1) has a formal solution of the form:

$$\Psi(t) = [\exp \left(-(i/\hbar) \, \mathcal{H}_0 t \right)] \, u \tag{1.8}$$

This equation has further implications. It tells us that the wave function can be separated into two parts, one time independent the other time dependent. This implies further that the wave equation is separable and one obtains the stationary wave equation, dependent only on space coordinates

$$\mathcal{H}_0 \mu = Eu \tag{1.9}$$

where E is the constant that is brought up by the separation of variables.

1*

Equation (1.9) is an eigenvalue equation. That is the operator $\mathscr{H}_0$ applied to the wave function u, produces the same wave function but multiplied by a constant. In the case of energy, we obtain an energy eigenvalue problem.

In fact an eigenvalue equation can be constructed from all observables, replaced by their proper operator equivalent. In general we have,

$$[\text{operator}] \text{ acting on} \begin{bmatrix} \text{wave} \\ \text{function} \end{bmatrix} = \begin{bmatrix} \text{measured} \\ \text{value} \end{bmatrix} \times \begin{bmatrix} \text{wave} \\ \text{function} \end{bmatrix}$$

In the case where the hamiltonian $\mathscr{H}_0$ is the operator, and where V has spherical symmetry, equation (1.9) can be separated into two equations. This is done by assuming a solution of the form

$$u = R(r)\, Y(\theta, \varphi) \tag{1.10}$$

where we use a spherical coordinates system. If we consider the interaction between a nucleus of charge Ze, mass M and an electron of charge e, mass m_e, we obtain the two following equations in which λ is the constant of separation of variables.

Radial part:

$$-\frac{\hbar^2}{2\mu r^2} \frac{d}{dr}\left(r^2 \frac{dR}{dr}\right) + \left[V(r) + \frac{\lambda \hbar^2}{2\mu r^2}\right] R = ER \tag{1.11}$$

Angular part:

$$-\frac{1}{\sin\theta} \frac{\partial}{\partial\theta}\left(\sin\theta \frac{\partial Y}{\partial\theta}\right) - \frac{1}{\sin^2\theta} \frac{\partial^2 Y}{\partial\varphi^2} = \lambda Y \tag{1.12}$$

where μ is the reduced mass $m_e M/(m_e + M)$ and $V(r)$ is $(-Ze^2/r)$. The wave functions that satisfy equation (1.12) are the spherical harmonics.

$$Y_{lm}(\theta\varphi) = N_{lm} P_l^m (\cos\theta) \exp(im\varphi) \tag{1.13}$$

where the P_l's are the legendre polynomials and N_{lm} is a factor that depends only on parameters l and m. The eigenvalues are $\lambda = l(l+1)$ which amounts to the statement that:

$$\mathbf{L}^2 Y_{lm}(\theta\varphi) = l(l+1)\, \hbar^2 Y_{lm}(\theta\varphi) \tag{1.14}$$

where $\mathbf{L}$ is the orbital angular momentum. The parameter l is called the orbital angular momentum quantum number; it can take values from $l = 0$ to $l = n - 1$ where n is a factor appearing in the solution of the radial equation. The parameter m is called the magnetic quantum number and gives the magnitude of L along a preferred axis called z axis

$$L_z Y_{lm}(\theta\varphi) = m_l\hbar Y_{lm}(\theta\varphi) \tag{1.15}$$

It can take values from $-l$ to $+l$.

The wave functions that satisfy equation (1.11) are of the form

$$R_{nl}(r) = N_{nl} \exp(-1/2\varrho)\,\varrho^l L_{n+l}^{2l+1}(\varrho) \tag{1.16}$$

where N_{nl} is a constant that depends only on l, n, and fundamental constants and where L_{n+l}^{2l+1} are the Laguerre polynomials. The variable ϱ is given by $\varrho = (2Z/na_0)\,r$, where a_0 is the radius of first Bohr orbit, $[a_0 = (\hbar^2/\mu e^2)]$. The possible values of E are given by

$$E_n = -\frac{\mu Z^2 e^4}{2\hbar^2 n^2} \tag{1.17}$$

The parameter n, the principal quantum number, may take integral values from 1 to ∞. Electronic spin does not appear explicitly in the Schrödinger representation. It appears naturally however in Dirac's relativistic theory. It can be treated like an angular momentum but with half integral quantum numbers. If $\mathbf{S}$ is the spin vector, then its lenght is given by $\sqrt{s(s+1)}\,\hbar$ where $s = 1/2$. Its projection on an axis of quantization is given by m_s taking values $\pm 1/2$ with corresponding eigenfunction $\Psi(\pm 1/2)$ usually denoted by α and β.

$$\mathbf{S}^2\Psi = s(s+1)\,\hbar^2\Psi \tag{1.18}$$

$$S_z\Psi = m_s\hbar\Psi \tag{1.19}$$

Angular momentum and spin add vectorially and it is convenient to define a total angular momentum $\mathbf{J}$, with quantum number j and projection m_j.

1.3 MATRIX REPRESENTATION

The stationary wave equation (1.9) lends itself naturally to a matrix representation in the following way.

Let us assume we have a set of functions u_n which is orthonormal and complete.

$$\int_{\text{all space}} u_n^* u_k \, d\tau = \delta_{nk} \tag{1.20}$$

The set is complete in the sense that any function can be expressed as a linear combination of the u_n's.

Let us assume further that each member of the set is an eigenfunction of $\mathscr{H}_0$ with eigenvalue E_n. Equation (1.9) can then be written as:

$$\mathscr{H}_0 u_n = E_n u_n \tag{1.21}$$

We can manipulate equation (1.21) in the following way. Multiply from the left by u_k^* and integrate over all space:

$$\int_{\text{all space}} u_k^* \mathscr{H}_0 u_n \, d\tau = E_n \int_{\text{all space}} u_k^* u_n \, d\tau \tag{1.22}$$

There are values on the right only for $k = n$ which implies that the only values of the integral on the left exist when $k = n$. Thus:

$$E_n = \int_{\text{all space}} u_n^* \mathscr{H}_0 u_n \, d\tau = \langle n | \mathscr{H}_0 | n \rangle \tag{1.23}$$

The last equation is in fact an expression of the third postulate.

Those members form an array from $n = 1$ to its maximum value. They can be used as the diagonal elements of a matrix which has the form:

base u:

$$\begin{pmatrix} \langle 1 | \mathscr{H}_0 | 1 \rangle & & 0 \\ & \langle 2 | \mathscr{H}_0 | 2 \rangle & \\ & & \langle 3 | \mathscr{H}_0 | 3 \rangle \\ 0 & & \langle n | \mathscr{H}_0 | n \rangle \end{pmatrix} = \begin{pmatrix} E_1 & & 0 \\ & E_2 & \\ & & E_3 \\ 0 & & E_n \end{pmatrix} \tag{1.24}$$

There is a unique equivalence between the left and right members of this equation and calculating the energy levels of the systems consists only in calculating the diagonal matrix elements of $\mathscr{H}_0$.

However there are cases where the eigenfunctions u_n are not known. Nevertheless we may still have at hand a set of functions v_n which is complete and orthonormal. The matrix elements of $\mathscr{H}_0$ can then be calculated with the v_n but the hamiltonian matrix will not be diagonal. We may have, for example, a matrix such as:

base v:

$$\begin{pmatrix} \langle 1 | \mathscr{H}_0 | 1 \rangle & \cdots & \langle 1 | \mathscr{H}_0 | n \rangle \cdots \\ & \text{etc.} & \\ \langle n | \mathscr{H}_0 | 1 \rangle & \cdots & \langle n | \mathscr{H}_0 | n \rangle \cdots \end{pmatrix} \tag{1.25}$$

We call v and u the basis functions for the representation of the hamiltonian $\mathcal{H}_0$. If u is a complete set, the function v can be expressed as a linear combination of the u's as in the following relation:

$$v_k = \sum_n b_{nk} u_n \tag{1.26}$$

The coefficients b_{kn} form a unitary matrix B and expression (1.26) is identical with the following matrix representation:

$$
\begin{bmatrix} v_1 \\ v_2 \\ v_3 \\ v_n \end{bmatrix} = \begin{bmatrix} b_{11} & b_{12} & \cdots & \\ & b_{22} & & \\ & & & \\ & & b_{kn} & \\ & b_{nk} & b_{nn} \end{bmatrix} \begin{bmatrix} u_1 \\ u_2 \\ u_3 \\ u_n \end{bmatrix} \tag{1.27}
$$

We may think of matrix B as transforming space u into a space v which can be used as the basis for representation of the operator $\mathcal{H}_0$. Since the u's are eigenfunctions of $\mathcal{H}_0$ the v's are not unless B is the unit matrix it follows that the matrix of $\mathcal{H}_0$ in basis v is not diagonal. The matrix, however, can be made diagonal by unitary transformation through the B matrix and we have:

$$(B\mathcal{H}_0^v B^{-1})_{kl} = E_k \delta_{kl} \tag{1.28}$$

which says that the transformation makes the matrix $\mathcal{H}_0^v$ diagonal with the elements equal respectively to E_l.

In a similar way, any operator may have a matrix representation in a given base. The choice of the set of basis functions is dictated by the problem at hand.

One of the most important variables in quantum mechanics is the total angular momentum which we have denoted by $\mathbf{J}$.

The angular momentum $\mathbf{J}$, is a vector and has a matrix representation. This means that each component in the xyz space has a matrix representation in multidimensional space whose unit vectors are the members of a complete set of wave functions which are orthonormal. The choice of these basis functions is made such as to make $\mathbf{J}^2$ and J_z diagonal with eigenvalues given by the following equations:

$$\mathbf{J}^2 |j, m\rangle = j(j + 1)\, \hbar^2 |j, m\rangle \tag{1.29}$$

$$J_z |j, m\rangle = m\hbar| j, m\rangle \tag{1.30}$$

where j is the angular momentum quantum number and m is the magnetic quantum number. The maximum value that can be taken by J_z is $j\hbar$.

The x and y components of angular momentum are not diagonal in the basis which makes J^2 and J_z diagonal. These matrices can be obtained from the definition of two very useful operators, J_+ and J_-:

$$J_x = \frac{1}{2}(J_+ + J_-) \tag{1.31}$$

$$J_y = \frac{1}{2i}(J_+ - J_-) \tag{1.32}$$

The properties of the J_+ and J_- operators acting on wave functions $|j, m\rangle$ for which J^2 and J_z have diagonal representation are:

$$J_+ |j, m\rangle = \hbar \sqrt{j(j + 1) - m(m + 1)}\, |j, m + 1\rangle \tag{1.33}$$

$$J_- |j, m\rangle = \hbar \sqrt{j(j + 1) - m(m - 1)}\, |j, m - 1\rangle \tag{1.34}$$

Table I

	$\frac{1}{2}$	$\frac{1}{2}$	1	1	1	$\frac{3}{2}$	$\frac{3}{2}$	$\frac{3}{2}$	$\frac{3}{2}$
j									
m	$\frac{1}{2}$	$-\frac{1}{2}$	1	0	-1	$\frac{3}{2}$	$\frac{1}{2}$	$-\frac{1}{2}$	$-\frac{3}{2}$
	$\frac{1}{2}$	0							
	0	$\frac{1}{2}$							
$J_z = \hbar$			1	0	0				
			0	0	0				
			0	0	-1				
						$\frac{3}{2}$	0	0	0
						0	$\frac{1}{2}$	0	0
						0	0	$-\frac{1}{2}$	0
						0	0	0	$-\frac{3}{2}$

Table I cont.

j	$\frac{1}{2}$	$\frac{1}{2}$	1	1	1	$\frac{3}{2}$	$\frac{3}{2}$	$\frac{3}{2}$	$\frac{3}{2}$
m	$\frac{1}{2}$	$-\frac{1}{2}$	1	0	-1	$\frac{3}{2}$	$\frac{1}{2}$	$-\frac{1}{2}$	$-\frac{3}{2}$
$J_x = \hbar$	0	$\frac{1}{2}$							
	$\frac{1}{2}$	0							
			0	$\frac{1}{\sqrt{2}}$	0				
			$\frac{1}{\sqrt{2}}$	0	$\frac{1}{\sqrt{2}}$				
			0	$\frac{1}{\sqrt{2}}$	0				
						0	$\frac{\sqrt{3}}{2}$	0	0
						$\frac{\sqrt{3}}{2}$	0	1	0
						0	1	0	$\frac{\sqrt{3}}{2}$
						0	0	$\frac{\sqrt{3}}{2}$	0

In table I the matrices J_z, J_x, and J_y for $j = 1/2, 1, (3/2)$ are given. Matrices for higher values of j can be calculated from equations (1.30), (1.33), and (1.34).

These matrices are very useful in evaluating transition probabilities between various levels in a given manifold of m_j under the perturbation of a r.f. field.

In connection with these matrices, the energy eigenvalues of a spin in a magnetic field H_z can be calculated with the help of equation (1.7). The hamiltonian becomes:

$$\mathscr{H}_0 = \mu_z H_z \qquad (1.35)$$

$$\mathscr{H}_0 = \gamma \hbar J_z H_z \qquad (1.36)$$

where γ is the gyromagnetic ratio.

Table I cont.

j	$\frac{1}{2}$	$\frac{1}{2}$	1	1	1	$\frac{3}{2}$	$\frac{3}{2}$	$\frac{3}{2}$	$\frac{3}{2}$
m	$\frac{1}{2}$	$-\frac{1}{2}$	1	0	-1	$\frac{3}{2}$	$\frac{1}{2}$	$-\frac{1}{2}$	$-\frac{3}{2}$
$J_y = \hbar$	0	$-\frac{i}{2}$							
	$\frac{i}{2}$	0							
			0	$-\frac{i}{\sqrt{2}}$	0				
			$\frac{i}{\sqrt{2}}$	0	$-\frac{i}{\sqrt{2}}$				
			0	$\frac{i}{\sqrt{2}}$	0				
						0	$\frac{i\sqrt{3}}{2}$	0	0
						$\frac{i\sqrt{3}}{2}$	0	$-i$	0
						0	i	0	$-\frac{i\sqrt{3}}{2}$
						0	0	$\frac{i\sqrt{3}}{2}$	0

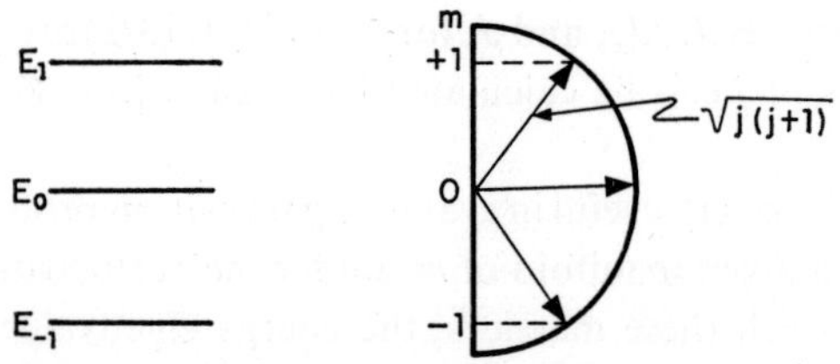

Figure 1.1 A magnetic moment μ in a magnetic field has discrete energy levels given by $\gamma \hbar m H_z$. The diagram shown is for the case $j = 1$

Using the basis which makes J_z diagonal, it follows that the matrix representing $\mathscr{H}_0$ is diagonal; the elements are given by:

$$\langle m \,|\mathscr{H}_0|\, m \rangle = \gamma \hbar m H_z \qquad (1.37)$$

In writing these three equations, of course, we assume that the magnetic field does not connect the states inside the manifold concerned to other states in another manifold in the same atom. In other words, we assume that the $|m\rangle$ wave functions form a complete orthonormal set in the manifold J, not connected to other sets by the perturbation. A frequent case is a free electron in a magnetic field with angular momentum $|J_z| = 1/2\hbar$ and with energy $\pm(\gamma\hbar H_z/2)$.

Important other properties of the J_i components are:

$$J_x J_y - J_y J_x = iJ_z\hbar \tag{1.38}$$

$$J_y J_z - J_z J_y = iJ_x\hbar \tag{1.39}$$

$$J_z J_x - J_x J_z = iJ_y\hbar \tag{1.40}$$

Another important property of those angular momentum operators is their hermiticity. In general an operator A is said to be hermitian when

$$A_{nn'} = A^*_{n'n} \tag{1.41}$$

where $A_{nn'}$ is a matrix element of A in a given representation. All operators representing physical observables are hermitian. A glance at the matrix representation of the J_i's shows clearly that property.

1.4 COUPLING OF ANGULAR MOMENTUM

We have chosen a set of basis vectors to form a space in which we could represent individual angular momentum components. In the case where two angular momenta are coupled to form a given system, a representation can be found in which, J^2, the total angular momentum of the two angular momenta added vectorially, and J_z, the projection of J on an axis z, are diagonal. The basis vectors of that representation are linear combinations of the product wave functions of the individual angular momenta. The coefficients of each term of that linear combination, giving such a representation for J_z and J^2, are called either Glebsch Gordon, Wigner or angular momentum coupling coefficients. The final basis vectors $U(JM_J)$ are given in terms of the original uncoupled basis vectors that we call v and u for each angular momentum respectively. The relation connecting the u's, v's and U's is:

$$U(JM_J) = \sum C(JM_J, m_1 m_2) \times v(j_1, m_1) \times u(j_2, m_2) \tag{1.42}$$

The coefficients C form a matrix and are given in Appendix 1, up to $j_1 = 1/2$ and $j_2 = 3/2$.

1.5 ROTATION OF FRAMES IN QUANTUM MECHANICS

We would like now to relate the above concepts to the rotation of axis formalism which we encounter in the study of magnetic resonance.

The phenomenon of magnetic resonance is best studied in a mathematical formalism of a rotating frame of coordinates. Suppose we have a spin I with magnetic moment μ in a magnetic field H_0; we know that this spin precesses around the direction of the field at an angular frequency given by:

$$\omega_0 = \gamma H_0 \ (Lamor\ frequency) \tag{1.43}$$

The phenomenon of resonance is obtained by applying a rotating magnetic field of amplitude H_1 at right angle to H_0.

As on figure 1.2 we can attach to this vector H_1 a frame of reference rotating at the angular velocity ω of the field:

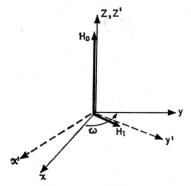

Figure 1.2   Rotating frame of reference attached to a rotating field component H_1

In the rotating frame, the motion of the magnetic moment may then be described by defining an effective field H_{eff}:

$$\frac{D\mu}{Dt} = \mu \times \gamma \mathbf{H}_{\text{eff}} \tag{1.44}$$

where

$$\mathbf{H}_{\text{eff}} = \mathbf{k}' \left(H_0 + \frac{\omega}{\gamma} \right) + H_1 \mathbf{i}' \tag{1.45}$$

At resonance $\omega = \omega_0 = \gamma H_0$ and the observer in the rotating frame sees only the presence of the field H_1. For that observer, μ precesses around H_1 at an angular velocity:

$$\omega_1 = \gamma H_1 \tag{1.46}$$

In the rotating frame, we may think of that last equation in term of a Larmor precession of μ around H_1.

The rotation operator

In order to describe rotation of axis in quantum mechanics, it is convenient to define a rotation operator $R_z(\alpha)$ in terms of the z components of angular momentum. We shall now derive such an operator.

The *xyz* coordinates under a rotation α around the *z* axis, transform according to the rule:

$$\begin{pmatrix} x' \\ y' \\ z' \end{pmatrix} = \begin{pmatrix} \cos\alpha & \sin\alpha & 0 \\ -\sin\alpha & \cos\alpha & 0 \\ 0 & 0 & 1 \end{pmatrix} \begin{pmatrix} x \\ y \\ z \end{pmatrix} \tag{1.47}$$

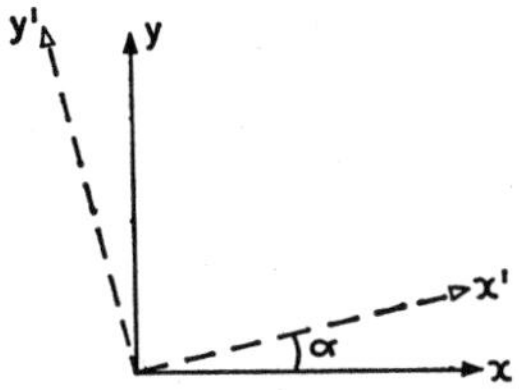

Figure 1.3 Definition of the rotation α in the *xy* plane

For an infinitesimal rotation $d\alpha$ we can, of course, write the matrix of rotation as:

$$\begin{pmatrix} x' \\ y' \\ z' \end{pmatrix} = \begin{pmatrix} 1 & d\alpha & 0 \\ -d\alpha & 1 & 0 \\ 0 & 0 & 1 \end{pmatrix} \begin{pmatrix} x \\ y \\ z \end{pmatrix} \tag{1.48}$$

This means that the matrix applied on our system of axis rotates it by an infinitesimal amount $d\alpha$ around the z axis.

Consequently, a function of *xyz* under an infinitesimal rotation $d\alpha$ transforms according to:

$$R(d\alpha)f(xyz) = f(x + (d\alpha)\,y, \, y - (d\alpha)\,x, \, z) \tag{1.49}$$

This can be expanded in a Taylor series:

$$R(d\alpha)f = f(xyz) + (d\alpha)\,y\,\frac{\partial f}{\partial x} - (d\alpha)\,x\,\frac{\partial f}{\partial y} + \cdots \tag{1.50}$$

$$= \left[1 + d\alpha\left(y\,\frac{\partial}{\partial x} - x\,\frac{\partial}{\partial y} \right) \right] f(xyz) \tag{1.51}$$

From the classical definition of angular momentum and the postulates of quantum mechanics formulated earlier, we can write the z components of the angular momentum J as:

$$J_z = -i\hbar\left(x\frac{\partial}{\partial y} - y\frac{\partial}{\partial x}\right) \qquad (1.52)$$

We define:

$$I_z = \frac{J_z}{\hbar} = i\left(y\frac{\partial}{\partial x} - x\frac{\partial}{\partial y}\right) \qquad (1.53)$$

This expression replaced in equation (1.53) gives:

$$R(d\alpha)f(xyz) = [1 - iI_z\,d\alpha]f(xyz) \qquad (1.54)$$

I_z is called the infinitesimal rotation operator. We may pass to a finite rotation through the following trick. Say α is the rotation wanted. We can do it in m steps; m being a large number, we write $d\alpha = \alpha/m$ and we can write:

$$R(\alpha) = \lim_{m\to\infty}\left[1 - iI_z\frac{\alpha}{m}\right]^m \qquad (1.55)$$

Using the binomial expansion one obtains

$$= \lim_{m\to\infty}\left[1 - i\alpha I_z + \frac{m(m-1)}{2!}\left(\frac{i\alpha I_z}{m}\right)^2 - \cdots\right] \qquad (1.56)$$

$$= 1 - i\alpha I_z + \left[\frac{(i\alpha I_z)^2}{2!} - \frac{(i\alpha I_z)^3}{3!} + \cdots\right] \qquad (1.57)$$

$$R(\alpha) = \exp\left(-i\alpha I_z\right) \qquad (1.58)$$

where the last form is a symbolic one which means the series of equation (1.57). Whenever we shall want to apply $R(\alpha)$ to a function we will have to take care of the properties of I_z as an operator and consequently go through the expansion.

Schrödinger equation in rotating coordinates

The relation between Ψ in the fixed frame of reference and Ψ_r in a frame rotating at angular velocity ω around the z axis is:

$$\Psi = \exp\left(-i\omega I_z t\right)\Psi_r \qquad (1.59)$$

Schrödinger's equation for a spin I in a magnetic field H which may contain a time dependent part is:

$$i\hbar\frac{\partial\Psi}{\partial t} = -\gamma\hbar\mathbf{I}\,.\,\mathbf{H}\Psi \qquad (1.60)$$

with Ψ above we have:

$$i\hbar\left[-i\omega I_z \exp(-i\omega I_z t)\Psi_r + \exp(-i\omega I_z t)\frac{\partial \Psi_r}{\partial t}\right]$$
$$= -\gamma\hbar\mathbf{I}\cdot\mathbf{H}\exp(-i\omega I_z t)\Psi_r \qquad (1.61)$$

We multiply from the left by $\exp(i\omega I_z t)$ and obtain

$$i\hbar\frac{\partial \Psi_r}{\partial t} = -\gamma\hbar\left\{\frac{\omega}{\gamma}I_z + \exp(i\omega I_z t)\mathbf{I}\cdot\mathbf{H}\exp(-i\omega I_z t)\right\} \qquad (1.62)$$

In the case of a field formed of a constant field H_0 along the z axis and a rotating field H_1 in the xy plane we have:

$$\mathbf{H}(t) = \mathbf{i}H_1\cos\omega t + \mathbf{j}H_1\sin\omega t + \mathbf{K}H_0 \qquad (1.63)$$

The interaction can then be written

$$\mathbf{I}\cdot\mathbf{H} = I_z H_0 + \exp(-iI_z\omega t)I_x\exp(iI_z\omega t)H_1 \qquad (1.64)$$

Replacing in the above expression, we obtain:

$$i\hbar\frac{\partial \Psi_r}{\partial t} = -\gamma\hbar\left\{\frac{\omega}{\gamma}I_z + \exp(i\omega I_z t)[I_z H_0 + \exp(-iI_z\omega t)I_x\right.$$
$$\left. \times \exp(iI_z\omega t)H_1]\exp(-i\omega I_z t)\right\} \qquad (1.65)$$

Using the expansion of I_z, we obtain:

$$= -\gamma\hbar\mathbf{I}\cdot\mathbf{H}_{\mathrm{eff}}\Psi_r \qquad (1.66)$$

where

$$\mathbf{H}_{\mathrm{eff}} = \mathbf{k}'\left(\frac{\omega}{\gamma} + H_0\right) + \mathbf{i}'H_1 \qquad (1.67)$$

which is the effective field in the classical model of magnetic resonance.

1.6 TIME INDEPENDENT PERTURBATION THEORY

In many cases the hamiltonian is independent of time. When there are several interactions that take place it is possible to arrange them in order of magnitude. Suppose we have $\mathscr{H}_{op}$ consisting of $\mathscr{H}_0$ large and $\mathscr{H}'$ small. It is then possible to find a set of basis vectors that will make $\mathscr{H}_0$ diagonal in a particular matrix representation, as we have shown before. However $\mathscr{H}'$ may not be diagonal in that particular basis, and in the matrix representing $(\mathscr{H}_0 + \mathscr{H}')$ off-diagonal elements with small values appear. We may then have something of the form

$$
\begin{pmatrix}
E_1^0 + \langle 1 |\mathscr{H}'| 1\rangle & \langle 1 |\mathscr{H}'| 1\rangle & \langle 1 |\mathscr{H}'| 3\rangle & \cdots \\
\langle 2 |\mathscr{H}'| 1\rangle & E_2^0 + \langle 2 |\mathscr{H}'| 2\rangle & \langle 2 |\mathscr{H}'| 3\rangle & \cdots \\
\langle 3 |\mathscr{H}'| 1\rangle & \langle 3 |\mathscr{H}'| 2\rangle & E_3^0 + \langle 3 |\mathscr{H}'| 3\rangle & \cdots \\
& \cdot \quad \cdot \quad \cdot &
\end{pmatrix} \qquad (1.68)
$$

where

$$
E_n^0 = \langle n| \mathscr{H} |n\rangle \cdots \text{etc.} \cdots
$$

A correction to the energy E_n^0 may be made *in first order* simply by considering the effect of the diagonal elements of $\langle n| \mathscr{H}' |n\rangle$. In many cases this is sufficient. For example, in the case the E_n's are separated by an energy corresponding to several GHz and the perturbation $\mathscr{H}'$ correspond to an interaction of the order of a few kilocycles, not much error is made in taking account of the diagonal elements only. The energy is then given by

$$
E_n^1 = E_n^0 + \langle n |\mathscr{H}'| n\rangle \qquad (1.69)
$$

A second order correction to the energy may be made by taking into account the effect of the off-diagonal elements. In that case the energy is given by

$$
E_n^2 = E_n^0 + \langle n |\mathscr{H}'| n\rangle + \sum_k \frac{|\langle n |\mathscr{H}'| k\rangle|^2}{E_k - E_n} \qquad (1.70)
$$

It is very seldom necessary to go to perturbations of higher orders in the problems in which we are interested.

The wave function can be also corrected to first order and second order. However for a second order correction the formula is quite involved and is not much of interest to us. In first order, the wave function is given by

$$
\Psi_n' = \Psi_0 + \sum_k \frac{\langle k| \mathscr{H}' |n\rangle}{E_k - E_n} \Psi_k \qquad (1.71)
$$

The degenerate case in which some energy values of $\mathscr{H}_0$ are equal in zero order is somewhat special since the correction to the wave function in first order tends to infinity. It is however possible some times to divide the matrix into blocks which are not directly interconnected. In those cases one can apply a rotation to the basis vectors, which makes those blocks diagonal and which removes the degeneracy. That situation is the one most often encountered specially when the interaction is of the magnetic type*.

1.7 TIME DEPENDENT PETURBATION THEORY

In the case $\mathcal{H}_{op}$ is a time dependent hamiltonian we have to use equation (1.1) making the solution to the problem much more involved. However, $\mathcal{H}_{op}$ consists normally of a static part $\mathcal{H}_0$ very large and a time dependent part $\mathcal{H}_1$ rather small. In that case, the solution of the problem is much simplified; actually a perturbation calculation is sufficient in most cases to give us the results needed. In that context, equation (1.1) can be written:

$$(\mathcal{H}_0 + \mathcal{H}_1)\Psi = i\hbar \frac{\partial}{\partial t}\Psi \tag{1.72}$$

Without the perturbation, we have:

$$\mathcal{H}_0 u_n = E_n u_n \tag{1.73}$$

where the u_n's form a complete orthonormal set of eigenfunctions of $\mathcal{H}_0$ with eigenvalue E_n. In that case, the perturbed function can be expanded in terms of those zero order wavefunctions. We thus write as a solution of equation (1.72), a wave function of the form:

$$\Psi = \sum_n a_n u_n \tag{1.74}$$

We replace that last expansion in equation (1.56), multiply on the left by u_k^*, integrate over all space and obtain:

$$\frac{d}{dt}a_k = -\frac{i}{\hbar}E_k a_k - \frac{i}{\hbar}\sum_n \langle k|\mathcal{H}_1|n\rangle a_n \tag{1.75}$$

We may simplify further by taking:

$$a_k = c_k \exp\left[-(i/\hbar)E_k t\right] \tag{1.76}$$

This is called the interaction representation which we will study in detail later in connection with the time dependence of the density matrix elements.

---

* For a more elaborate treatment of the time independent perturbation theory the reader is referred to standard textbooks on quantum mechanics listed at the end of the present monograph.

When equation (1.60) is replaced into equation (1.59), we obtain:

$$\frac{d}{dt} c_k = -\frac{i}{\hbar} \sum_n \langle k | \mathscr{H}'_1 | n \rangle c_n \qquad (1.77)$$

where

$$\mathscr{H}'_1 = \exp\left[(i/\hbar) E_k t\right] \mathscr{H}_1 \exp\left[-(i/\hbar) E_n t\right] \qquad (1.78)$$

We will have a chance to come back later on the meaning of that last equation. We will prove in fact that equation (1.78) expresses $\mathscr{H}_1$ in a frame of reference rotating at the angular frequency $(E_k - E_n)/\hbar$.

Equation (1.77) is the key to the problem of finding the effect of a small time dependent perturbation on a system such as an atom. In fact, the true problem starts there; since $|c_k|^2$ is the probability of finding the particle in state k, integration of equation (1.77) over the time of application of the perturbation should give the information wanted. However such an integration is not always easy to perform owing to the complicated form that $\mathscr{H}_1$ can take. On the other hand, in chapter 3 and 4 we shall see that we actually can get rather simple solutions of (1.77) for ensembles of particles in particular cases, and we shall not get farther here in this subject. It should be sufficient to realize that in principle equation (1.77) can be integrated:

$$c_k = -\frac{i}{\hbar} \int_0^t \sum_n \langle k | \mathscr{H}'_1 | n \rangle c_n \qquad (1.79)$$

and will give the information on the wave function Ψ which is the function describing the system.

This book is in a sense oriented around the solution of equation (1.77) for an ensemble of particles in various physical environments.

CHAPTER 2

The Density Matrix Formalism

THE REST OF this book is devoted entirely to a study of the density matrix formalism and its application to solving various problems related to quantum electronics. The present chapter introduces the concept of the density matrix in a somewhat formal way. However, the physical meaning of the various equations is given as often as it is possible in terms of measurable physical parameters.

2.1 MAGNETIZATION OF AN ENSEMBLE OF PARTICLES

One of the most illustrative examples in the subject of magnetism is the calculation of Curie's law from concepts on microscopic properties of matter. The idea is simple. One starts from the concept of a micromagnet on the atomic scale, expresses mathematically the distribution of N of those magnets among the energy levels by Boltzmann statistics, and obtains the famous law:

$$M_z = \chi_0 H_z = \frac{Ng^2\beta^2 H_z}{3kT} j(j + 1) \tag{2.1}$$

where χ_0 is the susceptibility, H_z the magnetic field, g the splitting factor, j the angular momentum, k Boltzmann constant, T the temperature and β Bohr or nuclear magneton, depending on the case at hand. In this expression the Boltzmann factor has been linearized in energy for high temperatures. These semiclassical calculations give a result in agreement with experiment. It is even possible to obtain the complete expression without high temperature approximation and to make clear the effect of saturation at high fields. This is fine as long as one calculates M_z, that is, the magnetization along the magnetic field assumed in the z direction. The method does not work however for calculating M_x or M_y, the magnetization at right angle to M_z.

Classicaly, one knows that at equilibrium M_x and M_y are zero; this result is assumed on the basis that the phase of any micromagnet is random relative to its neighbors. The components of each micromagnet add along the z direction but cancel themselves in the xoy-plane due to their random phases as illustrated in figure 2.1.

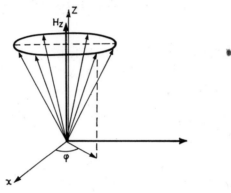

Figure 2.1 N micromagnets of random phase in a magnetic field H_z produce a net resultant M_z and no components in the xoy-plane

To be specific let us say that each micromagnet corresponds to the measurable magnetic properties of the spin of an electron. The spin angular momentum of the electron obeys the law

$$\mathbf{S}^2\psi = s(s + 1)\,\hbar^2\psi \tag{2.2}$$

where s is the spin quantum number and has the value $\frac{1}{2}$. To this angular momentum corresponds a magnetic moment given by:

$$\boldsymbol{\mu} = g\beta\mathbf{S} = \hbar\mathbf{S}\gamma \tag{2.3}$$

The magnetic moment can take only two directions with projection on an axis of quantization given, say, by a magnetic field H_z:

$$\mu_z = g\beta m \tag{2.4}$$

where $m = \pm\frac{1}{2}$ correspond to two energy states $E(\pm\frac{1}{2}) = \pm\frac{1}{2}g\beta H_z$.

This semiclassical picture of the spin of the electron is represented in quantum mechanics through the following concepts. Let us call Ψ the wave function of the electron spin:

$$|\Psi\rangle = a_{1/2}|+\tfrac{1}{2}\rangle + a_{-1/2}|-\tfrac{1}{2}\rangle \tag{2.5}$$

where $a_{1/2}$ is the amplitude of the component of the wave function Ψ for state $m = +\frac{1}{2}$, and $a_{-1/2}$ the amplitude of Ψ for state $m = -\frac{1}{2}$. Now if one calculates the components of the magnetization M_z, M_x, and M_y, one has to calculate the expectation values according to the formula:

$$\langle M_z \rangle = \langle \Psi | N\mu_z | \Psi \rangle \qquad (N = \text{total number of particles}) \qquad (2.6)$$

$$= \langle \Psi | N\gamma\hbar S_z | \Psi \rangle \qquad (2.7)$$

$$= \langle a_{1/2}|+\tfrac{1}{2}\rangle + a_{-1/2}|-\tfrac{1}{2}\rangle |N_y\hbar S_z| a_{1/2}|+\tfrac{1}{2}\rangle + a_{-1/2}|-\tfrac{1}{2}\rangle \qquad (2.8)$$

According to the diagonal properties of S_z in the representation used we have:

$$\langle M_z \rangle = \tfrac{1}{2}\gamma\hbar N[|a_{1/2}|^2 - |a_{-1/2}|^2] \qquad (2.9)$$

In that expression, $(a_{1/2})^2$ and $(a_{-1/2})^2$ are respectively the probability of occupation of the two levels $E_{1/2}$ and $E_{-1/2}$. The difference of probability is given by Boltzmann statistical law; for high temperatures, one obtains equation (2.1) with $S = \frac{1}{2}$. The calculation of M_x and M_y can be done in a similar way but it is more illustrative to calculate:

$$M_+ = M_x + iM_y \qquad (2.10)$$

$$M_- = M_x - iM_y \qquad (2.11)$$

$$\langle M_+ \rangle = \langle \Psi | N\mu_+ | \Psi \rangle \qquad (2.12)$$

$$= \langle \Psi | N\gamma\hbar(S_x + iS_y) | \Psi \rangle \qquad (2.13)$$

$$= N\gamma\hbar a_{1/2}^* a_{-1/2} \qquad (2.14)$$

Similarly for M_- one obtains

$$M_- = N\gamma\hbar a_{-1/2}^* a_{1/2} \qquad (2.15)$$

However we know that at equilibrium M_x and M_y are zero. To realize that result one would have to set either $a_{-1/2}$ or $a_{+1/2}$ equal to zero; this in turn, means complete polarization which violates the starting assumption of Boltzmann statistical equilibrium among the levels. In other words, by setting one of the a's equal to zero, one has to set the other equal to 1 to conserve the total number of particles, a law which is evident in the present cases. Thus, this simple point of view does not hold when we want to calculate the x or y components of the magnetization. The error in this reasoning comes from the fact that we assume, in drawing our conclusions, that all the spins have the same wave function or in other words the a's are equal for all spins. However, if we assume that the a's are not identical for all spins or if we associate a phase with the amplitudes, we can write that the average of the products $(a^*_{1/2} \times a_{-1/2})$ over the ensemble of particles is zero. That is:

$$\overline{\overline{a^*_{1/2}a_{-1/2}}} = 0 \qquad (2.16)$$

where the double bar means the average over the ensemble. As far as the square of those amplitudes are concerned the phase factors disappear and we have:

$$\overline{\overline{|a_{\pm 1/2}|^2}} = \frac{1}{N} \sum_i |a^i_{\pm 1/2}|^2 \qquad (2.17)$$

Thus, the description of an ensemble of particles with spins S by relative populations of the energy levels is not sufficient. The off-diagonal elements of the magnetization matrix would be deleted by such a narrow point of view. It is those off-diagonal elements which are responsible for all the interesting effects observed in the phenomena of magnetic resonance. The density matrix is just a formalism that takes care of that problem in an easy and natural way.

2.2 STATISTICAL ENSEMBLES

In the following chapters we will deal with large numbers of identical particles and we are interested to know the behaviour of these particles. In our context, however, all the characteristics or properties of the individual particles are not completly known; consequently we assume that these particles or systems form an ensemble which obeys statistical laws and on which averaging operations can be performed. This permits us the writing of mean properties for the ensemble, properties which characterize each system.

We are forced into statistical methods because, very often, we do not have enough information about the particular system we are interested in. If the state of the system is not completely determined, a weighing factor must be associated with the various possible states in which the system can be; in that case we say that we have a mixed state.

In the previous section, in order to obtain a null magnetization in the xy-plane at equilibrium, we have been obliged to assume that the various particles did not have all the same wave functions. Say we have a wave function

$$\Psi = a_1 u_1 + a_2 u_2 \qquad (2.18)$$

As it was shown in the case of equilibrium we must have $\overline{\overline{a_1^* a_2}}$ equal to zero. This is a normal situation met in practice. However, there are situations in which, for example, the phases of the a_i's are correlated or perhaps all the particles are in state 1 giving $a_1 = 1$ and $a_2 = 0$ for all particles; those situations are called pure states. For example the last case described is that of a completly polarized ensemble, in which a particle can be found in state 1 with certainty. That, of course, is not a normal situation and relaxation processes tend to distribute the particles among the levels and reestablish statistical equilibrium in the ensemble. That kind of equilibrium exists when the distribution of the systems among the states does not change with time; it is normally a Boltzmann type of distribution. In many cases which will concern us however, we shall assume that at equilibrium the difference of population between the levels is so small that for all purposes the levels are equally populated. (See appendix B).

2.3 THE STATISTICAL OPERATOR ϱ

We have introduced in section 1.1 Schrödinger's equation, have separated it into a time dependent part and a static part. We have found in particular that the static equation gave us the opportunity to build a fictitious space in which the vectors u_n being orthogonal are taken as the unit basis vectors. It is then possible to represent the state of a particle as a linear combination of those basis vectors with expansion coefficients a_n. In relation to our precedent discussion it is then possible to write the wave function of a pure state as:

$$\Psi = \sum_n a_n u_n \qquad (2.19)$$

In that context, the density matrix is a representation of the statistical operator ϱ in the u space. The operator contains all the information necessary for the description of a statistical ensemble of identical particles. The mathematical expression is (see appendix C for other definitions):

$$\boxed{\varrho_{nm} = \overline{\overline{a_m^* a_n}}} \qquad (2.20)$$

where the double bar means ensemble average. It is possible to define the operator ϱ in other ways. For example, the weighing factor associated with the possible states may be written explicitly as it is done in appendix C. The coefficients $\overline{\overline{a_n a_m^*}}$ conveniently arranged in rows and columns form a matrix and it is this matrix that we call the "density matrix". A very simple interpretation appears when one considers only the diagonal terms. In that case:

$$\varrho_{nn} = \overline{\overline{a_n a_n^*}} \tag{2.21}$$

The values of these elements give the probability of finding a system in the nth state. As mentioned in the previous section, we normally assume that the probability must obey Boltzmann law; the diagonal elements multiplied by the total number of particles give the population of the levels.

It is best to think of ϱ as an operator which, when acting on an eigenfunction u_n produces a linear combination of all the $u_n's$.

$$\varrho u_m = \sum_n \varrho_{nm} u_n \tag{2.22}$$

The elements of ϱ expressed in matrix form can then be written naturally as:

$$\boxed{\varrho_{nm} = \langle n| \varrho |m\rangle} \tag{2.23}$$

Of course, it should be understood that these elements are the same as those given by equation (2.20). In this connexion we say that the operator ϱ has a matrix representation in u space, whose elements are given by equation (2.23). The vectors u form then the basis of the representation.

2.4 EXPECTATION VALUES OF AN OPERATOR

Let us calculate the expectation value of an operator Q. This operator can be, for example, any components of angular momentum, magnetization or other measurable peoperties of an atomic system. By definition, the expectation value of Q is for a system:

$$\langle Q \rangle = \int \Psi^* Q \Psi \, d\tau \tag{2.24}$$

$$= \int \left(\sum_m a_m^* u_m^*\right) Q \left(\sum_n a_n u_n\right) d\tau \tag{2.25}$$

$$= \sum_m \sum_n a_m^* a_n \langle m| Q |n\rangle \tag{2.26}$$

For an ensemble, we average over all the systems:

$$\overline{\langle Q \rangle} = \sum_m \sum_n \overline{\overline{a_m^* a_n}} \langle m| Q |n\rangle \tag{2.27}$$

Using definition (2.20), we have:

$$\overline{\langle Q \rangle} = \sum_m \sum_n \varrho_{nm} \langle m| Q |n \rangle \tag{2.28}$$

which can be written:

$$\overline{\langle Q \rangle} = \sum_m \sum_n \langle n| \varrho |m \rangle \langle m| Q |n \rangle \tag{2.29}$$

$$= \sum_n \langle n| \varrho Q |n \rangle \tag{2.30}$$

$$\boxed{\overline{\langle Q \rangle} = \text{Tr}\, \varrho Q \equiv \text{Tr}\, Q \varrho} \tag{2.31}$$

where ϱ and Q are the matrices representing the operators ϱ and Q, and Tr means "take the trace or add all the diagonal elements of the matrix (ϱQ)". Thus, in that formalism, the expectation value of an operator averaged over the ensemble is obtained simply by making the product of the matrix of the operator and of the density matrix and taking the trace of the result. In a later section we will calculate the components of the magnetization which will illustrate this procedure.

2.5 PROPERTIES OF ϱ

1) ϱ IS A HERMITIAN OPERATOR   By definition, an operator ϱ is hermitian when:

$$\varrho_{nm} = \varrho_{mn}^* \tag{2.32}$$

This means that an operator is hermitian when the matrix representing this operator is equal to the matrix formed by changing rows and columns and taking the complex conjugate. We have defined:

$$\varrho_{nm} = \overline{a_m^* a_n} \tag{2.33}$$

This implies:

$$\varrho_{mn} = \overline{a_n^* a_m} \tag{2.33a}$$

which verify equation (2.32). The statistical operator ϱ is thus a hermitian operator. The same conclusion can be obtained by considering the fact that, if Q is a hermitian operator, we must have $\overline{\langle Q \rangle}$ real. This implies that ϱ is hermitian too.

2) THE OPERATOR UNITY (1)   We have:

$$\langle 1 \rangle = 1 = \mathrm{Tr}\,(1\varrho) = \mathrm{Tr}\,\varrho \qquad (2.34)$$

This implies:

$$\sum_n \varrho_{nn} = 1 \qquad (2.35)$$

or the sum of the diagonal elements must be unity. The physical meaning of this is that the probability of finding the systems in the states is unity. Or, since the diagonal elements represent the population normalized to unity, the total number of particles is conserved.

3) SIGN OF ϱ_{mn} Operators with nonnegative eigenvalues must have nonnegative mean values. That, in term, requires through equation (2.31), that ϱ must be positive or

$$\varrho_{kk} > 0 \qquad (2.36)$$

4) CHANGE OF REPRESENTATION   The matrix ϱ defined above is expressed in the representation u_n. This means that we have a complete set of orthonormal vectors u_n and that we form an n dimensional space with those vectors. Suppose now that we have another space formed with eigenvectors ϕ_k which are linear combinations of the u's:

$$\phi_k = \sum_n b_{nk} u_n \qquad (2.37)$$

The density matrix ϱ expressed in the u-representation can be transformed to the Φ representation in the following way. The elements of ϱ in basis Φ are:

$$\varrho_{nm}\phi = \int \phi_n^* \varrho \phi_m \, d\tau \qquad (2.38)$$

$$= \int \sum_k b_{kn}^* u_k^* \varrho \sum_e b_{en} u_e \, d\tau \qquad (2.39)$$

$$= \sum_k \sum_e b_{kn}^* \varrho_{ke}^u b_{en} \qquad (2.40)$$

$$\varrho_{nm}^\Phi = \sum_k \sum_e b_{nk}^* \varrho_{ke}^u b_{en} \qquad (2.41)$$

$$\varrho^\Phi = B^+ \varrho^u B \qquad (2.42)$$

where we have used the capital letters to represent symbolically the matrices of transformation and B^+ is the adjoint of B. The method of transformation from one representation to another amounts simply to a matrix multiplication. The calculation of the transformation matrix is a problem in itself. We shall consider it in specific cases later on connexion with spin exchange problems. In that case, we will pass freely from S to F representation and conversely, making use extensively of the Clebsch Gordon coefficients.

In general, we shall deal with transformation matrices for which their adjoints are equal to their inverses (unitary matrices). Thus, $B^+ = B^{-1}$ and from now on we shall use the transformation:

$$\varrho^\Phi = B^{-1} \varrho^u B \tag{2.43}$$

As a consequence of the possibility of transforming the matrix ϱ to another representation, it is possible to find a unitary transformation which will make ϱ diagonal. It amounts to a rotation of axes in the u-space.

2.6 SYSTEMS IN THE PRESENCE OF EACH OTHER

Suppose we have two systems interacting with each other and having eigenstates u_n and v_k. These two systems, for example, could be atoms making collisions with each other. We want to know how we should express the combined density matrix of the whole ensemble composed of systems a and b.

The expectation value of the operator products $Q^a Q^b$ can be written:

$$\langle Q^a Q^b \rangle = \int \sum_n a_n^* u_n^* \sum_k b_k^* v_k^* Q^a Q^b \sum_m a_m u_m \sum_e b_e v_e \, d\tau \tag{2.44}$$

$$\langle Q^a Q^b \rangle = \sum_n \sum_k \sum_m \sum_e a_n^* a_m b_k^* b_e \int u_n^* v_k^* Q^a Q^b u_m v_e \, d\tau \tag{2.45}$$

In several cases that will interest us, the vectors u and v are independant of each other. It is then possible to write:

$$\int u_n^* v_k^* Q^a Q^b u_m v_e \, d\tau = \int u_n^* Q^a u_m \, d\tau_a \int v_k^* Q^b v_e \, d\tau_b = \langle n | Q^a | m \rangle \langle k | Q^b | e \rangle \tag{2.46}$$

The grand average of $\langle Q^a Q^b \rangle$ can thus be written according to (2.31):

$$\overline{\langle Q^a Q^b \rangle} = \mathrm{Tr} \, [\varrho^{ab} Q^{ab}] \tag{2.47}$$

where

$$\varrho^{ab} = \varrho^a \times \varrho^b \tag{2.48}$$

$$Q^{ab} = Q^a \times Q^b \tag{2.49}$$

where the sign " $\times$ " means a direct product raising the orders of the matrices to the product of the order of each matrix. The reader should be aware of the rapidly raising complexity in such problems. For example, in the study of spin exchange interactions in atomic hydrogen collisions the order of the resultant matrices representing transformation of operators is $4 \times 4 = 16$; but, in rubidium 87, one has to deal with matrices of order $8 \times 8 = 64$. Fortunately, in most cases we are interested only in traces and the problem is much reduced.

2.7   TIME DEPENDENCE OF ϱ

We would like to find a general equation that governs the time variation of ϱ. We shall do this in the most general case where the hamiltonian of the system $\mathcal{H}$ may depend itself on time. In this general case, Schrödinger equation is:

$$-\frac{\hbar}{i} \frac{\partial}{\partial t} \Psi = \mathcal{H} \Psi \tag{2.50}$$

Suppose we have a complete set of vectors u_n. For example, it is often possible to write $\mathcal{H}$ as made of two parts; one time independent called $\mathcal{H}_0$ and one time dependent called $\mathcal{H}_1$. The vectors u_n could then be eigenfunctions of $\mathcal{H}_0$ with energy values E_n. There is no restriction here on the relative magnitude of $\mathcal{H}_1$ and $\mathcal{H}_0$. However, in most experimental situations, $\mathcal{H}_1$ is much smaller than $\mathcal{H}_0$.

We thus write:

$$\Psi = \sum_n a_n u_n \tag{2.51}$$

and substitute in equation (2.50):

$$-\frac{\hbar}{i} \frac{\partial}{\partial t} \sum_n a_n u_n = \sum_n a_n \mathcal{H} u_n \tag{2.52}$$

Multiply from the left by u_k and integrate over all space; this gives:

$$\frac{\partial}{\partial t} a_k = (i\hbar)^{-1} \sum_n a_n \langle k| \mathcal{H} |n\rangle \tag{2.53}$$

$$\frac{\partial}{\partial t} a_k^* = -(i\hbar)^{-1} \sum_n a_n^* [\langle k| \mathcal{H} |n\rangle]^* \tag{2.54}$$

On the other hand we have:

$$\frac{d}{dt} a_m^* a_n = a_m^* \frac{da_n}{dt} + \frac{da_m^*}{dt} a_n \tag{2.55}$$

Replacing equations (2.53) and (2.54) into equation (2.55), we have, using the proper notation

$$= (i\hbar)^{-1} \sum_i (a_m^* a_i \mathscr{H}_{ni} - a_i^* a_n \mathscr{H}_{im}) \qquad (2.56)$$

where $\mathscr{H}$ is a hermitian operator. Averaging over the ensemble of systems and using the definition of the density matrix elements formulated earlier we obtain:

$$\frac{d}{dt} \varrho_{nm} = (i\hbar)^{-1} \sum_i (\mathscr{H}_{ni} \varrho_{im} - \varrho_{ni} \mathscr{H}_{im}) \qquad (2.57)$$

This equation can be written formally:

$$\boxed{\frac{d\varrho}{dt} = (i\hbar)^{-1} [\mathscr{H}, \varrho]} \qquad (2.58)$$

This is the fundamental equation in the formalism. Owing to the general form of $\mathscr{H}$ we can apply that equation to any ensemble. However, $\mathscr{H}$ can take a very complicated form in the most simple situations and this will limit us in the solution of equation (2.58) to cases where $\mathscr{H}$ can be written partly as a large $\mathscr{H}_0$ constant in time and a small time dependent $\mathscr{H}_1$.

When $\mathscr{H}_1$ is zero equation (2.58) becomes:

$$\frac{d\varrho}{dt} = (i\hbar) [\mathscr{H}_0, \varrho] \qquad (2.59)$$

In the case the basis vectors u are eigenfunctions of $\mathscr{H}_0$ we have

$$\sum_i \langle n| \mathscr{H}_0 |i\rangle = E_n \qquad (2.60)$$

$$\sum_i \langle i| \mathscr{H}_0 |m\rangle = E_m \qquad (2.61)$$

which makes:

$$\frac{d\varrho_{nm}}{dt} = (i\hbar)^{-1} \varrho_{nm}(E_n - E_m) \qquad (2.62)$$

This has for solution:

$$\varrho_{nm}(t) = \exp \left[-i/\hbar(E_n - E_m) t \right] \varrho_{nm}(0) \qquad (2.63)$$

In the case of the diagonal elements we have $E_n = E_m$ and

$$\varrho_{nm}(t) = \varrho_{nn}(0) = \text{constant} \qquad (2.64)$$

This reflects the statistical nature of our physical ensembles. Although, there can be a lot of particles transferred from one level to another, even in equilibrium, the net effect on the average population is nil since the relative populations of the levels stay constant in time. However, this is not true about the off-diagonal elements. Equation (2.63) does not say that off-diagonal elements exists, but it says that if we can define an origin of time $t = 0$ when we have $\varrho_{nm}(t) = \varrho_{nm}(0)$, then $\varrho_{nm}(t)$ will be time dependent according to the law (2.63).

In the case of spins $\frac{1}{2}$ in a magnetic field H_z the E_i are given by:

$$E_i = \pm\tfrac{1}{2}g\beta H_z \tag{2.65}$$

The Larmor frequency being:

$$\omega_0 = \frac{E_n - E_m}{\hbar} = \frac{g\beta H_z}{\hbar} \tag{2.66}$$

we can write equation (2.63):

$$\varrho_{nm}(t) = \varrho_{nm}(0) \exp\left(-i\omega_0 t\right) \tag{2.67}$$

It says that the off-diagonal elements if they exist oscillate in time at the Larmor frequency.

2.8 TIME DEPENDENCE OF OPERATORS AVERAGED OVER THE ENSEMBLE

We have found earlier that the expectation value of an operator Q averaged over an ensemble could be written as the trace of the product of the matrices ϱ and Q. We would like to find the actual dependence of Q on time.

We take again as our starting point Schrödinger equation, however with $\mathscr{H}_0$ constant:

$$-\frac{\hbar}{i}\frac{\partial}{\partial t}\Psi = \mathscr{H}_0\Psi \tag{2.68}$$

A formal solution of this equation is:

$$\Psi(t) = \exp\left[-(i/\hbar)\,\mathscr{H}_0 t\right]\Psi(0) \tag{2.69}$$

We can expand $\Psi(0)$ in terms of a complete set of vectors u_n which are not necessarily eigenfunctions of $\mathscr{H}_0$:

$$\Psi(0) = \sum_n c_n u_n \tag{2.70}$$

where the u_n's and c_n's are independent of time. The expectation value of the operator Q can then be written as:

$$\langle Q \rangle = \int \left[\sum_n \exp\left[-(i/\hbar)\, \mathscr{H}_0 t\right] c_n u_n \right]^* Q \left[\sum_m \exp\left[-(i/\hbar)\, \mathscr{H}_0 t\right] c_m u_m \right] d\tau$$

(2.71)

$$= \int \sum_n \sum_m c_n^* c_m u_n^* \exp\left[(i/\hbar)\, \mathscr{H}_0 t\right] Q \exp\left[-(i/\hbar)\, \mathscr{H}_0 t\right] u_m \, d\tau \qquad (2.72)$$

For the average over the ensemble we obtain:

$$\overline{\langle Q \rangle} = \sum_n \sum_m \varrho_{mn}(0) \int u_n^* \exp\left[+(i/\hbar)\, \mathscr{H}_0 t\right] Q \exp\left[-(i/\hbar)\, \mathscr{H}_0 t\right] u_m \, d\tau$$

(2.73)

$$= \mathrm{Tr}\, \varrho(0)\, Q(t) \qquad (2.74)$$

where

$$Q(t) = \exp\left[(i/\hbar)\, \mathscr{H}_0 t\right] Q(0) \exp\left[-(i/\hbar)\, \mathscr{H}_0 t\right] \qquad (2.75)$$

However, the time dependence explicit in $Q(t)$ can be transferred to ϱ in the following way. Equation (2.73) can be written with the help of equation (2.23):

$$\overline{\langle Q \rangle} = \sum_n \sum_m \langle m|\, \varrho(0)\, |n\rangle \langle n|\, \exp\left[(i/\hbar)\, \mathscr{H}_0 t\right] Q \exp\left[-(i/\hbar)\, \mathscr{H}_0 t\right] |m\rangle$$

(2.76)

Using the property of close sets $\sum_{n'} |n'\rangle \langle n'| = 1$ we can write:

$$\overline{\langle Q \rangle} = \sum_n \sum_m \sum_{m'} \sum_{n'} \langle m|\, \varrho(0)\, |n\rangle \langle n|\, \exp\left[(i/\hbar)\, \mathscr{H}_0 t\right] |n'\rangle$$

$$\langle n'|\, Q\, |m'\rangle \langle m'|\, \exp\left[-(i/\hbar)\, \mathscr{H}_0 t\right] |m\rangle \qquad (2.77)$$

The factors $\langle i|\, \exp\left[\pm(i/\hbar)\, \mathscr{H}_0 t\right]|j\rangle$ being matrix elements, thus numbers can be transferred anywhere in the summation:

$$\overline{\langle Q \rangle} = \sum_n \sum_m \sum_{n'} \sum_{m'} \langle m'|\, \exp\left[-(i/\hbar)\, \mathscr{H}_0 t\right] |m\rangle \langle m|\, \varrho(0)\, |n\rangle$$

$$\langle n|\, \exp\left[(i/\hbar)\, \mathscr{H}_0 t\right] |n'\rangle \langle n'|\, Q\, |m'\rangle \qquad (2.78)$$

Using the properties of the summation we thus obtain:

$$\overline{\langle Q \rangle} = \mathrm{Tr}\, (\varrho(t)\, Q(0)) \qquad (2.79)$$

where $Q(0)$ is independent of time;

and
$$\varrho(t) = \exp\left[-(i/\hbar)\,\mathscr{H}_0 t\right]\varrho(0)\exp\left[(i/\hbar)\,\mathscr{H}_0 t\right] \qquad (2.80)$$

This equality has a very significative physical meaning. It says that one can either attach the time dependence to the vectors u of the expansion (2.70), or to the coefficients c. In the u-space, it amounts effectively to rotation of the basis vectors or to rotation of the wave function $\Psi(0)$ itself through time variation of the c's. With that reasoning, it becomes evident that operators which have a matrix representation in this base will vary in time according to equation (2.79) since

$$\exp\left[(i/\hbar)\,\mathscr{H}_0 t\right]$$

can be thought of as a unitary transformation of the representation. The same remarks are true about ϱ which has a representation in u-space given by equation (2.23), and equation (2.80), could, in fact, have been written at once.

When the vectors u_n are chosen such as to be eigenfunctions of $\mathscr{H}_0$, some of the relations given above becomes trivial since elements like

$$\langle m|\exp\left[-(i/\hbar)\,\mathscr{H}_0 t\right]|m\rangle \quad \text{become} \quad \exp\left[-(i/\hbar)\,E_m t\right]$$

E_m being no longer an operator. We shall see later the implication of this in connexion with the components of angular momentum in real space.

CHAPTER 3

Effects of Perturbations on the Density Matrix

IN THIS CHAPTER we shall consider the effect of perturbations on the elements of the density matrix ϱ. These perturbations may be of a coherent type, like that produced by the application of a r.f. field on an ensemble of spins, or may be of the random type like relaxation or optical pumping in specific cases. This chapter is a general introduction to the various phenomena and specific problems that will be studied later.

The basic equation is equation (2.58) and we shall use it extensively. It gives us a handle to manipulate ϱ with various perturbations applied on the ensemble. In fact, equation (2.58) is the equation that makes clear the phenomenon of coherence that may exist in the ensemble. By that we mean that the application of a coherent perturbation which may drive the ensemble at a given frequency ω_0 will be reflected in the solution of equation (2.58). In fact, due to the phenomenon of coherence, off-diagonal elements in the matrix appear; those are time dependent and their effects can be detected by simple experiments on the ensemble. This is where we see the difference from the study of standard magnetic resonance where one looks at the effect of a r.f. field on a particular spin or magnetic moment in a d.c. magnetic field. In that case, the spin is assumed to be pointing in a particular direction or in other words is assumed in a pure state. Here we take the whole ensemble, represent the statistical distribution of its constituents in various sub-levels, and look at the effect of the r.f. field on this ensemble. The situation is somewhat reversed, then, from the standard magnetic resonance methods. It is easy to see that in standard magnetic resonance analysis where we deal in most cases with the effect of perturbations on the populations, we are missing something. Bloch equations take care of this situation by assuming phenomenologically the presence of right angle components in the magnetization matrix. These components however, appear naturally in the density matrix formalism whenever the perturbations produce coherence in the physical system.

3.1 INTERACTION REPRESENTATION

We found in the last chapter that the operator ϱ obeys the equation:

$$d\varrho/dt = (i\hbar)^{-1} (\mathscr{H}\varrho - \varrho\mathscr{H}) \qquad (3.1)$$

In the case $\mathscr{H}$ is independent of time, this equation has a formal solution:

$$\varrho(t) = \exp\left[-(i/\hbar)\,\mathscr{H}_0 t\right] \varrho(0) \exp\left[(i/\hbar)\,\mathscr{H}_0 t\right] \qquad (3.2)$$

The elements of the density matrix can then be calculated through equation (3.2) by standard techniques used earlier. Of course, if the basic vectors chosen for the representation of ϱ are eigenfunctions of $\mathscr{H}_0$, the results obtained are that of equation (2.63), which makes clear the time dependence of the off-diagonal elements of ϱ.

Let us now assume that the Hamiltonian $\mathscr{H}$ can be written in the form:

$$\mathscr{H} = \mathscr{H}_0 + \mathscr{H}_1 \qquad (3.3)$$

where $\mathscr{H}_0$ $\cdots$ time independent
$\quad\;\;\mathscr{H}_1$ $\cdots$ time dependent

If $\mathscr{H}_1$ is small we should expect that equation (3.2) is an approximate solution of equation (3.1). However we can still do better. Suppose we write:

$$\varrho(t) = \exp\left[-(i/\hbar)\,\mathscr{H}_0 t\right] \varrho'(t) \exp\left[(i/\hbar)\,\mathscr{H}_0 t\right] \qquad (3.4)$$

where $\varrho'(t)$ contains the variation in time due to $\mathscr{H}_1$. In other words if $\mathscr{H}_1$ was much smaller than $\mathscr{H}_0$, $\varrho'(t)$ would not change much during the time of one full cycle of the exponential and equation (3.4) would be a logical solution to equation (3.1). However we do not limit the relative values of $\mathscr{H}_0$ and $\mathscr{H}_1$ and try equation (3.4) as a solution of equation (3.1). We differentiate equation (3.4) and replace in equation (3.1).

$$\exp\left[-(i/\hbar)\,\mathscr{H}_0 t\right]\frac{d\varrho'}{dt}\exp\left[(i/\hbar)\,\mathscr{H}_0 t\right] = (i\hbar)^{-1}\left[\mathscr{H}_1\varrho - \varrho\mathscr{H}_1\right] \qquad (3.5)$$

Multiplying from the left by $\exp\left[(i/\hbar)\,\mathscr{H}_0 t\right]$ and from the right by $\exp\left[-(i/\hbar)\,\mathscr{H}_0 t\right]$ and defining

$$\varrho'(t) = \exp\left[(i/\hbar)\,\mathscr{H}_0 t\right] \varrho(t) \exp\left[-(i/\hbar)\,\mathscr{H}_0 t\right] \qquad (3.6)$$

$$\mathscr{H}'_1(t) = \exp\left[(i/\hbar)\,\mathscr{H}_0 t\right] \mathscr{H}_1(t) \exp\left[-(i/\hbar)\,\mathscr{H}_0 t\right] \qquad (3.7)$$

we obtain finally the reduced form:

$$\boxed{\frac{d\varrho'}{dt} = (i\hbar)^{-1} [\varrho', \mathscr{H}'_1]}$$

(3.8)

That last equation describes the variation of ϱ in a new representation that we call the interaction representation. In fact we have separated the time effect of $\mathscr{H}_0$ and $\mathscr{H}_1$ by a simple mathematical approach. It is also seen that if $\mathscr{H}_1 = 0$, ϱ' is a constant of motion in that representation.

In this section we have effectively shown the basic difference between Schrödinger and Heisenberg representations. In the case u is an eigenfunction of $\mathscr{H}_0$, equations (2.51), (2.69) and (2.70) can be combined to give:

$$\Psi(t) = \sum_n a_n u_n = \sum_n c_n u_n \exp\left[-(i/\hbar) E_n t\right]$$

(3.9)

In Schrödinger representation we have:

$$\varrho_{mn} = \overline{a_n^* a_m}$$

(3.10)

In Heisenberg representation:

$$\varrho'_{mn} = \overline{c_n^* c_m}$$

(3.11)

Obviously the relation between the two representations is given by equation (3.4) which in the present case reduces to:

$$\varrho'_{mn} = \varrho_{mn} \exp\left[(i/\hbar) (E_m - E_n) t\right]$$

(3.12)

which agrees with our previous definitions.

From those definitions we see that our original definition of ϱ through equation (2.20) was done in the Schrödinger representation.

3.2 INTERACTION REPRESENTATION AS A ROTATION OF AXIS

We have seen that the formal solution of Schrödinger's equation in the case of a time independent hamiltonian is:

$$\Psi(t) = \exp\left[-(i/\hbar) \mathscr{H}_0 t\right] \Psi(0)$$

(3.13)

and that the expectation value of an operator Q is given by:

$$\langle Q \rangle = \mathrm{Tr}\, \varrho(0)\, Q(t)$$

(3.14)

where
$$Q(t) = \exp\left[(i/\hbar)\,\mathscr{H}_0 t\right] Q(0) \exp\left[-(i/\hbar)\,\mathscr{H}_0 t\right] \tag{3.15}$$

In the case of a spin I in a magnetic field along the z direction we can write:
$$\mathscr{H}_0 = -\gamma\hbar H_0 I_z \tag{3.16}$$
which makes:
$$\Psi(t) = \exp\left(i\omega_0 I_z t\right) \Psi(0) \tag{3.17}$$

$$Q(t) = \exp\left(-i\omega_0 t I_z\right) Q(0) \exp\left(-i\omega_0 t I_z\right) \tag{3.18}$$

In the case of angular momentum components we obtain:

$$I_{i'}(t) = \exp\left(-i\omega_0 t I_z\right) I_i(0) \exp\left(i\omega_0 t I_z\right) \tag{3.19}$$

We suspect that $I_{i'}$ is effectively $I_i(0)$ expressed in a system of axis rotated through the angle $\alpha = \omega_0 t$. This is easily seen through the relations we have derived earlier. However, we can show this directly by expanding the exponentials into their proper series for each component:

$$I_{x'} = \exp\left(-i\alpha I_z\right) I_x \exp\left(i\alpha I_z\right) \tag{3.20}$$

$$= \left(1 - i\alpha I_z + \frac{(-i\alpha I_z)^2}{2!} + \cdots\right)$$

$$\times I_x\left(1 + i\alpha I_z + \frac{(i\alpha I_z)^2}{2!} + \cdots\right) \tag{3.21}$$

Using the properties of the commutator written in the first chapter, one obtains the following series:

$$I_{x'} = I_x\left(1 - \frac{\alpha^2}{2} + \frac{\alpha^4}{4} + \cdots\right) + I_y\left(\alpha - \frac{\alpha^3}{3} + \cdots\right) \tag{3.22}$$

$$I_{x'} = I_x \cos\alpha + I_y \sin\alpha \tag{3.23}$$

We can derive similar expressions for:

$$I_{y'} = -I_x \sin\alpha + I_y \cos\alpha \tag{3.24}$$

$$I_{z'} = I_z \tag{3.25}$$

This shows without ambiguity that $I_{x'}$, $I_{y'}$ and $I_{z'}$ are the components of angular momentum I in a system of axes $\sum'$ rotated by the angle α relative to the system $\sum$. If α is a linear function of time as $\omega_0 t$, then the system $\sum'$ is a rotating system of axes with angular velocity ω_0. In this connexion the interaction representation describes the motion of variables in a system of axes rotating at angular velocity ω_0.

3.3 COHERENT AND RANDOM PERTURBATIONS

In the study of magnetic resonance, one is faced with the problem of studying the effects of several perturbations applied simultaneously. In most cases we have to deal with an aggregate of spins perturbed or driven coherently by a radio frequency wave while the individual spins are more or less violently disturbed by fluctuations in the environmental fields. The coherent radio frequency wave is normally applied to the system to probe the physical properties of the ensemble while the fluctuations in the environmental fields are perturbations we have to deal with and accept as they are; however, these fluctuations are in many cases most interesting to study and from their effects on the ensemble of spins a lot of informations can be obtained about the internal properties of matter.

In all cases of course we can use equation (3.1) which describe the general effect of a hamiltonian $\mathscr{H}$ on the density matrix. However for our purpose equation (3.8) is more tractable in the sense that we can investigate the effect of perturbations in a representation in which the effect of the time independent part of the hamiltonian is effectively not present. We have just seen, in connexion with the motion of a spin, that the interaction representation is actually one in which the frame of reference rotates in time at the Larmor frequency.

In a particular problem, we can develop equation (3.8) and write n equations for the n states at hand. We will have a chance to do that in the study of magnetic resonance and coherent atomic oscillators. It is, in fact, possible in certain cases to obtain exact solutions to problems which are not too complicated. However we would like to investigate here somewhat further the implications of that equation.

We have mentioned above the possibility of having coherent radiation applied on the system while fluctuations in the surroundings perturb the ensemble. It is convenient for this problem to divide the whole ensemble into several sub-ensembles, examine the effect of the various perturbations and then average over those sub-ensembles. It is possible through this procedure to differentiate between perturbations which introduce coherence in the ensemble and those which do not and even destroy such coherence when it is present. Before studying them, let us look at standard perturbation theory.

In the Heisenberg representation equation (2.53) can be written:

$$\frac{dc_k}{dt} = (ih)^{-1} \sum_n c_n \langle k| \mathscr{H}_1 |n\rangle \exp(i\omega_{kn}t) \tag{3.26}$$

where

$$\omega_{kn} = (1/\hbar)(E_k - E_n) \tag{3.27}$$

The formal solution of this equation can be obtained directly by integration. To do this we suppose one of the c_n's to be unity while all others are zero at $t = 0$. Then, equation (3.26) tells us what is the variation of the amplitude of state k with time under the effect of the perturbation $\mathscr{H}_1$ which we have not specified yet.

In that case we can write:

$$c_k = (i\hbar)^{-1} \int_0^t \langle k| \mathscr{H}_1(t') |n\rangle [\exp(-i\omega_{nk}t')] \, dt' \tag{3.28}$$

If the integration can be performed we can consider our problem as solved since we have the information on the coefficients which characterize the wave function of the problem at hand.

In practice as we have said earlier, we deal with ensembles and sub-ensembles; we need then to average the perturbation $\mathscr{H}_1(t)$ over the ensembles, and its value must be different from zero. Of course in the case of an r.f. field varying sinusoïdly, the perturbation is the same for all sub-ensembles and does not vanish. In that case we can calculate the elements $\langle k| \mathscr{H}_1(t') |n\rangle$ of the perturbation matrix and solve directly equation (3.8) or (3.26). Evidently, since in practice we measure the modules of the coefficients c_k both methods should give the same result. However equation (3.8) will give directly off-diagonal elements related to cross products of the c's.

There are perturbations, however, which do not introduce coherence into the system. Those are random perturbations and when averaged over the ensemble, they vanish:

$$\overline{\langle k| \mathscr{H}_1(t') |n\rangle} = 0 \tag{3.29}$$

For our purpose, we may define a random perturbation by that property. However, a random perturbation is normally defined as one whose value at each instant of time is a random variable which cannot be determined better than by a law of probability.

Although the average value of a perturbation is zero it may still have some effect on the ensemble. Standard perturbation theory will give the effects of such random perturbations on the populations of the levels through the following calculations.

The probability of occupation of a given level k is given by $c_k c_k^*$. Let us define a transition probability per unit time through the relation.

$$W_{kn} = \frac{d}{dt}(c_k c_k^*) \tag{3.30}$$

This gives us:

$$W_{kn} = c_k \frac{dc_k^*}{dt} + c_k^* \frac{dc_k}{dt} \tag{3.31}$$

which for an ensemble may be written:

$$W_{kn} = \frac{1}{\hbar^2} \int_0^t \overline{\langle n| \mathcal{H}_1(t) |k\rangle \langle k| \mathcal{H}_1(t') |n\rangle}$$

$$\times \{\exp[i\omega_{kn}(t' - t)]\}\, dt' + cc \tag{3.32}$$

If $\mathcal{H}_1(t)$ is a random perturbation, a function such as $\overline{\langle n| \mathcal{H}_1(t) |k\rangle \times \langle k| \mathcal{H}_1(t') |n\rangle}$ is called the auto-correlation function of $\mathcal{H}_1(t)$. In most cases we have to deal with stationary random perturbations which are those who are invariant under a change of origin of time. It is thus possible to write:

$$\tau = t - t' \tag{3.33}$$

and

$$G_{nk}(\tau) = \overline{\langle n| \mathcal{H}(t - \tau) |k\rangle \langle k| \mathcal{H}_1(t) |n\rangle} \tag{3.34}$$

as the auto-correlation function. The transition probability per unit time then becomes:

$$W_{kn} = \frac{1}{\hbar^2} \int_{-t}^t G_{nk}(\tau) [\exp(-i\tau\omega_{nk})]\, dt \tag{3.35}$$

where the complex conjugate part has been incorporated under the integration. The correlation function $G_{nk}(\tau)$ normally falls off for large τ; we then define a correlation time τ_c, such that $G_{nk}(\tau)$ is very small when $\tau \gg \tau_c$. We shall consider times much larger than τ_c and the integral can be written:

$$W_{kn} = \frac{1}{\hbar^2} \int_{-\infty}^{+\infty} G_{nk}(\tau) [\exp(-i\tau\omega_{nk})]\, d\tau \tag{3.36}$$

This equation can be recognized as the Fourier transform of $G_{nk}(\tau)$, the perturbation being:

$$J_{nk}(\omega_{nk}) = \int\limits_{-\infty}^{+\infty} G_{nk}(\tau) \left[\exp\left(-i\omega_{nk}\tau\right)\right] d\tau \tag{3.37}$$

We conclude from this calculation that the transition probability between two levels is proportional to the spectral density of the random perturbation at the frequency corresponding to resonance between those two levels.

Equation (3.36) gives us the rate of change of the population of the levels; it is a typical perturbation calculation. It shows us also that a random perturbation must have a high spectral density at the frequency of resonance between the levels in order to affect the populations. It should be noted also that the information obtained through equation (3.36) is quite restricted. It is not possible through this simple calculation to obtain information on the effect of perturbations on the coherence which could exist in an ensemble of atoms. For example, we could have an oscillating magnetization at right angle to a magnetic field. The calculation made above does not tell us how that magnetization disappears under the influence of a random perturbation. It tells us, however, the rate of decrease of the magnetization parallel to the d.c. field since this magnetization is proportional to the difference of populations of the energy levels.

To obtain such information relative to the coherence that may exist in an ensemble of particles, the best method is to integrate equation (3.8). We must recall that equation (3.8) has essentially been obtained through equation (2.55) which is very similar to equation (3.33) except for the fact that we have considered in the first case, cross products of the coefficients of probability. We can solve equation (3.8) by successive integration:

$$\varrho'(t) = \varrho'(0) + \frac{i}{\hbar} \int\limits_{0}^{t} \left[\varrho'(t')\,\mathscr{H}'_1(t')\right] dt' \tag{3.38}$$

where $\varrho'(0)$ is the value of ϱ at time $t = 0$. Replacing $\varrho'(t')$ by its value given by same equation we have:

$$\varrho'(t) = \varrho'(0) + \frac{i}{\hbar} \int\limits_{0}^{t} \left[\varrho'(0)\,\mathscr{H}'_1(t')\right] dt'$$

$$+ \left(\frac{i}{\hbar}\right)^2 \int\limits_{0}^{t'} \int\limits_{0}^{t} \left[\left[\varrho'(t'')\,\mathscr{H}'_1(t'')\right]\mathscr{H}'_1(t')\right] dt'\, dt'' \tag{3.39}$$

Since we are interested in most cases in the rate of change of $\varrho'(t)$ with time, we take the derivative of (3.39) with respect to time:

$$\frac{d\varrho'}{dt} = \frac{i}{\hbar} \left[\varrho'(0) \, \mathscr{H}'_1(t)\right]$$

$$+ \left(\frac{i}{\hbar}\right)^2 \int_0^t \left[[\varrho'(0) \, \mathscr{H}'_1(t')] \, \mathscr{H}'_1(t)\right] dt' \qquad (3.40)$$

where we have approximated $\varrho'(t')$ under the integral by $\varrho'(0)$, as is done in perturbation calculations.

We have not yet specified $\mathscr{H}'_1(t)$. In the case it is a random perturbation, its value vanishes when averaged over all the sub-ensembles, and we are left with:

$$\frac{d\varrho'}{dt} = \left(\frac{i}{\hbar}\right)^2 \int_0^t \left[[\varrho'(0) \, \overline{\mathscr{H}'_1(t')] \, \mathscr{H}'_1(t)}\right] dt' \qquad (3.41)$$

where ϱ' now stands for the whole ensemble. If we assume that $\varrho'_{kk}(0)$ is unity at time $t = 0$, and that a perturbation $\mathscr{H}'_1$ is connecting levels k and n we recognize easily equation (3.32) derived from standard perturbation theory. However equation (3.41) gives us more information; it actually tells us the effect of the perturbation on the off-diagonal elements of the density matrix, which are cross products of the c's and which we know are related to the coherence in the ensemble. Our tasks in the next section will be to calculate the value of the integral.

A very important case has been left out here. It is the case in which the perturbation hamiltonian consists at the same time of a random perturbation $\mathscr{H}'_1(t)$ and of a perturbation $\mathscr{H}'_2(t)$ introducing coherence in the system such as that produced by a radiation field varying sinusoïdally. Such a perturbation when averaged over the sub-ensembles does not vanish and the first term in equation (3.40) has to be considered. It is standard procedure to consider the effect of $\mathscr{H}'_2$ in the second term of this equation small compared to the first term. We thus neglect its effect in the integral and we write:

$$\frac{d\varrho'}{dt} = \frac{i}{\hbar} \left[\varrho'(0) \, \mathscr{H}'_2(t)\right]$$

$$+ \left(\frac{i}{\hbar}\right)^2 \int_0^t \left[[\varrho'(0) \, \overline{\mathscr{H}'_1(t')] \, \mathscr{H}'_1(t)}\right] dt' \qquad (3.42)$$

which amounts to saying that both perturbations act independently of each other.

One notices that the first term of equation (3.42) is exactly the same thing as equation (3.8) when the radiation field above is present. To obtain equation (3.8) we have done an approximation in passing from equation (3.2) to (3.4). This same trick may play again in our favour in changing $\varrho'(0)$ in the first term of (3.42) to $\varrho'(t)$. The above reasoning is not a proof that those approximations can be done. However it amounts to decouple entirely the various perturbations, to apply equation (3.8) successively for each of those perturbations and to add the results. Thus we write:

$$\frac{d\varrho'}{dt} = \sum_i^n \left(\frac{d\varrho'}{dt}\right)_i \qquad (3.43)$$

where n is the number of perturbations present.

3.4 RELAXATION

We have just devided perturbations into two main classes: perturbations which are of a random nature and those which are not random. The last type normally introduces coherence in the system while the first type destroys it.

The effect on the density matrix elements of a random perturbation can be expressed mathematically by a relaxation rate. This can be written in a phenomenological way as:

$$\frac{d\varrho_{\alpha\alpha}}{dt} = -\gamma_1\left(\varrho_{\alpha\alpha} - \frac{1}{n}\right) \qquad (3.44)$$

where n is the number of levels among which the particles are distributed and γ_1 is the population relaxation rate related to the longitudinal relaxation time of the Bloch formalism by the equation:

$$\gamma_1 = \frac{1}{T_1} \qquad (3.45)$$

In this context, equation (3.44) makes ϱ tend to an equal distribution of the particles among all states; that equation also assumes uniform relaxation among all the levels.

The off-diagonal elements of the density matrix are normally assumed to tend to zero at the rate γ_2:

$$\frac{d\varrho_{\alpha\alpha'}}{dt} = -\gamma_2(\varrho_{\alpha\alpha'}) \qquad (3.46)$$

where γ_2 is related to the transverse relaxation time through the equation:

$$\gamma_2 = \frac{1}{T_2} \qquad (3.47)$$

The physical problem is to calculate the rates γ_1 and γ_2 from first principles. In many instances, the problem is so complicated that one relies on experiments for their determination. However we can get general expressions for their values. Many authors have attacked that problem with more or less success. In fact, the reader may very well say at this time that we have already calculated γ_1 in the previous section. This is true indeed. However the calculation did not give us γ_2 which is most important in the case of coherent atomic oscillators since it determines the possibility of oscillations.

The values of γ_1 and γ_2 are hidden inside the complex integral of the right hand member of equation (3.42). Our task is to make explicit their values. In the interaction representation for a random perturbation, and for one of the sub-ensembles we have:

$$\frac{d\varrho'}{dt} = \left(\frac{i}{\hbar}\right)^2 \int_0^\tau \left[[\varrho'(0)\,\mathscr{H}'_1(t)]\,\mathscr{H}'_1(t)\right] dt' \qquad (3.48)$$

What we want is to obtain an expression for the variation of an element, say $\varrho_{\alpha\alpha'}$, as a function of all the other matrix elements. We can expand equation (3.48) in all the possible terms to obtain:

$$\begin{aligned}
\frac{d\varrho'_{\alpha\alpha'}}{dt} = \left(\frac{i}{\hbar}\right)^2 \int_0^t & \sum_\beta \sum_{\beta'} (\varrho'_{\alpha\beta}(0)\,\mathscr{H}'_1(t')_{\beta'\beta}\,\mathscr{H}_1(t)_{\beta\alpha'} \\
& - \varrho'_{\beta'\beta}(0)\,\mathscr{H}'_1(t')_{\alpha\beta'}\,\mathscr{H}'_1(t)_{\beta'\alpha'} \\
& - \varrho'_{\beta\beta'}(0)\,\mathscr{H}'_1(t)_{\alpha\beta}\,\mathscr{H}'_1(t')_{\beta'\alpha'} \\
& + \varrho'_{\beta'\alpha'}(0)\,\mathscr{H}'_1(t)_{\alpha\beta}\,\mathscr{H}'_1(t')_{\beta'\beta'}) \, dt' \qquad (3.49)
\end{aligned}$$

Actually writing our equation in this form is already solving it since we may easily recognize in the right hand side various combinations of the

ϱ's and products of $\mathscr{H}_1(t)$ at various times which we know will give us correlation functions. We can obtain a rather simple expression for equation (3.52) by writting explicitly $\mathscr{H}'_1(t)$ in Schrödinger's notation. We also define as we did earlier $\tau = t - t'$ and $E_\beta/\hbar = \beta$, etc... With this notation, we obtain:

$$\frac{d\varrho'_{\alpha\alpha'}}{dt} = \left(\frac{i}{\hbar}\right)^2 \sum_\beta \sum_{\beta'} \int_0^t d\tau$$

$$(\varrho'_{\alpha\beta'}\mathscr{H}_1(t-\tau)_{\beta\beta'}\mathscr{H}_1(t)_{\beta\alpha'}\, \exp\left[-i(\beta'-\beta)\tau\right]\exp\left[i(\beta'-\beta+\beta-\alpha')t\right]$$

$$- \varrho'_{\beta'\beta}\mathscr{H}_1(t-\tau)_{\alpha\beta'}\mathscr{H}_1(t)_{\beta\alpha'}\, \exp\left[-i(\alpha-\beta')\tau\right]\exp\left[i(\alpha-\beta'+\beta-\alpha')t\right]$$

$$- \varrho'_{\beta\beta'}\mathscr{H}_1(t)_{\alpha\beta}\,\mathscr{H}_1(t-\tau)_{\beta'\alpha'}\, \exp\left[-i(\beta'-\alpha')\tau\right]\exp\left[i(\beta'-\alpha'+\alpha-\beta)t\right]$$

$$+ \varrho'_{\beta'\alpha'}\mathscr{H}_1(t)_{\alpha\beta}\,\mathscr{H}_1(t-\tau)_{\beta\beta'}\, \exp\left[-i(\beta-\beta')\tau\right]\exp\left[i(\beta-\beta'+\alpha-\beta)t\right]$$

$$\tag{3.50}$$

We need to average the products of the perturbation over all the subensembles.
We define typically:

$$\overline{\mathscr{H}_1(t)_{\alpha\beta}\,\mathscr{H}_1(t+\tau)_{\beta'\alpha'}} = G_{\alpha\beta\alpha'\beta'}(\tau) \tag{3.51}$$

as one of the correlation function. We define also:

$$j_{\alpha\beta\alpha'\beta'}(\omega_{\alpha\beta}) = \int_0^\infty G_{\alpha\beta\alpha'\beta'}(\tau)[\exp(-i\omega_{\alpha\beta}\tau)]\,d\tau \tag{3.52}$$

Using the expansion of the exponentials in sine and cosine we can write that last expression as the sum of a real part and an imaginary part:

$$j_{\alpha\beta\alpha'\beta'}(\omega_{\alpha\beta}) = \tfrac{1}{2}\int_{-\infty}^{+\infty} G_{\alpha\beta\alpha'\beta'}(\tau)\,[\exp(-i\omega_{\alpha\beta}\tau)]\,d\tau$$

$$+ i\int_0^\infty G_{\alpha\beta\alpha'\beta'}(\tau)\,\sin\omega_{\alpha\beta}\tau\,d\tau \tag{3.53}$$

This first part (real) is recognized as the spectral density of $G_{\alpha\beta\alpha'\beta'}(t)$. The second part is imaginary; as we shall see later in connexion with spin exchange interactions an imaginary term in the relaxation mechanism gives rise to a small frequency shift. In general this shift is small and for all purposes where one is concerned with nuclear magnetic resonance in relatively broad lines, it can be neglected. However, in the case of atomic oscillators which have high precision and stability this shift may be detected.

We shall keep both terms and define:

$$j_{\alpha\beta\alpha'\beta'} = \tfrac{1}{2} J_{\alpha\beta\alpha'\beta'}(\omega_{\alpha\beta}) + i k_{\alpha\beta\alpha'\beta'}(\omega_{\alpha\beta}) \tag{3.54}$$

when $J_{\alpha\beta\alpha'\beta'}(\omega_{\alpha\beta})$ is the spectral density of the perturbation at the frequency $\omega_{\alpha\beta}$. Equation (3.50) averaged over the ensemble can then be written as:

$$
\begin{aligned}
\frac{d\varrho'}{dt} = \sum_{\beta}\sum_{\beta'} \left(\frac{i}{\hbar}\right)^2 & \delta_{\alpha\beta} \sum_{\gamma} \varrho'_{\beta\beta'} j_{\beta'\gamma\alpha'\gamma}(\omega_{\beta'\gamma}) \exp\left[i(\alpha - \beta - \alpha' + \beta')\,t\right] \\
& - \varrho'_{\beta\beta'} j_{\alpha\beta\alpha'\beta'}(\omega_{\alpha\beta}) \exp\left[i(\alpha - \beta - \alpha' + \beta')\,t\right] \\
& - \varrho'_{\beta\beta'} j_{\beta'\alpha'\beta\alpha}(\omega_{\beta'\alpha'}) \exp\left[i(\alpha - \beta - \alpha' + \beta')\,t\right] \\
& + \delta_{\alpha'\beta'} \sum_{\gamma} \varrho'_{\beta\beta'} j_{\gamma\beta\gamma\alpha}(\omega_{\gamma\beta}) \exp\left[i(\alpha - \beta - \alpha' + \beta')\,t\right]
\end{aligned}
\tag{3.55}
$$

where we have assumed that the integral extends over a time t much greater than the correlation time τ_c at which the value of the correlation function is small; consequently we have replaced t by ∞ as the limit of integration. In the case where we neglect the effect of the imaginary term, equation (3.55) can be written in a symbolic form:

$$\boxed{\frac{d\varrho'_{\alpha\alpha'}}{dt} = \sum_{\beta\beta'} R_{\alpha\alpha'\beta\beta'} \varrho'_{\beta\beta'} \exp\left[i(\alpha - \beta - \alpha' + \beta')\,t\right]} \tag{3.56}$$

where we have defined:

$$
\begin{aligned}
R_{\alpha\alpha'\beta\beta'} = \frac{1}{2\hbar^2} \Big\{ & J_{\alpha\beta\alpha'\beta'}(\omega_{\alpha\beta}) + J_{\alpha\beta\alpha'\beta'}(\omega_{\alpha'\beta'}) - \delta_{\alpha\beta} \sum_{\gamma} J_{\gamma\alpha'\gamma\beta'}(\omega_{\gamma\beta'}) \\
& - \delta_{\alpha'\beta'} \sum_{\gamma} J_{\gamma\beta\gamma\alpha}(\omega_{\gamma\beta}) \Big\}
\end{aligned}
\tag{3.57}
$$

The coefficients $R_{\alpha\alpha'\beta\beta'}$ are of course relaxation rates in the general sense. Equation (3.56) can be further simplified by noting that the exponential is a factor varying very rapidly. In all cases we shall consider only terms in which:

$$\alpha - \alpha' = \beta - \beta'$$

which makes the exponential equal to unity.

The theory just developed is known as Redfield's theory of relaxation. It is one of the most general ones, relative to this subject, relating in a simple way the variation of one of the ϱ's to all the others through a set of coefficients $R_{\alpha\alpha'\beta\beta'}$. Of course equation (3.57) is just another form of equation (3.48) averaged over the ensemble. We have effectively displaced the problem to a calculation of the spectral densities; on the other hand the J terms are not easy to calculate and in most cases we must rely on the experiments to give us their values. In the case of diagonal elements equation (3.55) reduces to the master equation for relaxation:

$$\frac{d\varrho'_{\alpha\alpha}}{dt} = \frac{1}{\hbar^2} \sum_{\beta} \left(J_{\beta\alpha}(\omega_{\beta\alpha}) \varrho'_{\beta\beta} - J_{\alpha\beta}(\omega_{\beta\alpha}) \varrho'_{\alpha\alpha} \right) \tag{3.58}$$

where the J's are generally proportional to the spin lattice relaxation times.

CHAPTER 4

Magnetism and Magnetic Resonance

THE THEORY DEVELOPED in the preceding section finds a most beautiful application in the solution of problems related to magnetic resonance. This section covers this subject and we shall apply our formalism to basic phenomena such as stimulated emission, $\pi/2$ and π pulses, relaxation and spin echoes.

4.1 EFFECT OF A COHERENT R.F. FIELD ON THE DENSITY MATRIX

In order to study the phenomenon of magnetic resonance let us place ourselves in the most simple situation. For that, we will take the case of an ensemble of spins of angular momentum $I = \frac{1}{2}$ which, for the present, are assumed to have negligible interaction between themselves. This could be the case of protons in water. This will permit us to obtain a very simple density matrix for an ensemble of spins under the influence of coherent radiation but not of relaxation. The calculation is very illustrative of later application in the theory of masers. It is assumed that a field H_0 is present and is in the z direction. In the general case I, we recall

$$E_m = \langle m | \mathscr{H}_0 | m \rangle \tag{4.1}$$

$$= \langle m | \gamma \hbar H_0 I_z | m \rangle \tag{4.2}$$

$$= \gamma \hbar H_0 m = \hbar \omega_0 m \tag{4.3}$$

with the definition:

$$\omega_0 = \gamma H_0 \tag{4.4}$$

the Larmor frequency as in classical language or the angular frequency of precession of the spins around the z axis. Let us say that we apply on our ensemble of spins an oscillating magnetic field of the form:

$$H_x(t) = 2H_1 \cos \omega t \tag{4.5}$$

This field could be produced by a coil or a cavity in which we force a given current. The amplitude factor is written $2H_1$ for the following reason. A field oscillating linearly can be decomposed into two counter-rotating field components of the same amplitude H_1 which can be written:

$$H_{rot} = iH_1 \cos \omega t + jH_1 \sin \omega t \qquad (4.6)$$

By chosing the sign of ω, we can either have the right or left hand sense of rotation. If ω is close to ω_0, the frequency of precession of the magnetic moment, there will be an interaction with one of those components. This can be written:

$$\mathscr{H}_1 = \gamma \hbar H_1 (I_x \cos \omega t + I_y \sin \omega t) \qquad (4.7)$$

Using the definition of sine and cosine in terms of exponentials and

$$I_+ = I_x + iI_y$$
$$I_- = I_x - iI_y \qquad (4.8)$$

we can write

$$\mathscr{H}_1 = \frac{\gamma \hbar H_1}{2} [I_+ \exp(-i\omega t) + I_- \exp(i\omega t)] \qquad (4.9)$$

The matrix elements of this last hamiltonian reflect transitions up or down.

$$\langle m | \mathscr{H}_1 | m - 1 \rangle = \frac{\gamma \hbar H_1}{2} \sqrt{(I + m)(I - m + 1)} \exp(-i\omega t) \qquad (4.10)$$

$$\langle m - 1 | \mathscr{H}_1 | m \rangle = \frac{\gamma \hbar H_1}{2} \sqrt{(I + m)(I - m + 1)} \exp(+i\omega t) \qquad (4.11)$$

The effect of this perturbation on the density matrix can be calculated through equation (2.58). In the case $I = 1/2$, in a magnetic field H_0 we have two levels:

$$E_{\pm 1/2} = \pm \tfrac{1}{2} \hbar \omega_0 \qquad (4.12)$$

The variation of the elements of ϱ are given in Schrödinger's representation by:

$$i\hbar \frac{d}{dt} \varrho_{mn} = \sum_i (\mathscr{H}_{mi} \varrho_{in} - \varrho_{mi} \mathscr{H}_{in}) \qquad (4.13)$$

The matrix elements of $\mathscr{H}$ are:

$$\mathscr{H}_{ni} = \langle n | (\mathscr{H}_0 + \mathscr{H}_1) | i \rangle \qquad (4.14)$$

where

$$\langle n | \mathscr{H}_0 | i \rangle = E_n \delta_{ni} \qquad (4.15)$$

and where $\langle n | \mathscr{H}_1 | i \rangle$ is given by equation (4.10) and (4.11). We recall the definition

$$\gamma H_1 = \omega_1 \tag{4.16}$$

which, for the present calculations, is assumed constant over the ensemble of atoms or spins. Later, we shall consider cases where H_1 is not constant over the ensemble and we shall have to perform averages. Evaluating the matrix elements (4.10) and (4.11) for the case $I = \frac{1}{2}$ we obtain the following set of equations:

$$\frac{d\varrho_{11}}{dt} = \omega_1 \times \text{Im}\, \varrho_{21} \exp\left(-i\omega t\right) \tag{4.17}$$

$$\frac{d\varrho_{22}}{dt} = -\omega_1 \times \text{Im}\, \varrho_{21} \exp\left(-i\omega t\right) \tag{4.18}$$

$$\frac{d\varrho_{21}}{dt} = i\omega_0\varrho_{21} - \frac{i\omega_1}{2}(\varrho_{11} - \varrho_{22}) \exp\left(i\omega t\right) \tag{4.19}$$

For the case where the frequency applied ω is equal to the precession frequency ω_0, we have a simple solution in matrix form. The origin of time is chosen such that at $t = 0$, $\varrho_{11} = 1$ and $\varrho_{22} = 0$. We also make $\varrho_{21}(0) = 0$.

$$\varrho(t) = \begin{pmatrix} \dfrac{\cos \omega_1 t + 1}{2} & \dfrac{i}{2} \sin \omega_1 t \exp\left(-i\omega_0 t\right) \\[3mm] -\dfrac{i}{2} \sin \omega_1 t \exp\left(i\omega_0 t\right) & \dfrac{1 - \cos \omega_1 t}{2} \end{pmatrix} \tag{4.20}$$

It is seen from this result that the application of a perturbation which is coherent creates off-diagonal elements in the density matrix. Those off-diagonal elements reflect the coherence introduced into the system and we shall see later, in connexion with the calculation of the magnetization, the physical meaning of those off-diagonal elements. The off-diagonal elements vary in amplitude according to $\sin \omega_1 t$ where ω_1 is a precession frequency of the magnetization around the rotating vector H_{rot}; those off-diagonal elements oscillate also at the frequency ω_0 which is the Larmor frequency of the spins.

We have obtained the solution of our problem in Schrödinger's representation. However we could as well work it out in the interaction representation. We then have to use as our starting point equation (3.8) written here explicitly:

$$(i\hbar)\frac{d\varrho'_{mn}}{dt} = \sum_i (\mathcal{H}'_{Ini}\varrho'_{im} - \varrho'_{ni}\mathcal{H}'_{Iim}) \tag{4.21}$$

The solution of the set of equations that result is done in a method similar to the one used above and we obtain, at resonance:

$$\varrho'(t) = \begin{pmatrix} \dfrac{\cos\omega_1 t + 1}{2} & \dfrac{i}{2}\sin\omega_1 t \\[3mm] -\dfrac{i}{2}\sin\omega_1 t & \dfrac{-\cos\omega_1 t + 1}{2} \end{pmatrix} \tag{4.22}$$

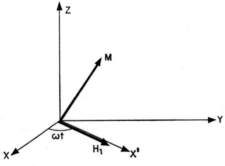

Figure 4.1 In the interaction representation, at resonance, the magnetization appears to precess around H_1 at the frequency ω_1

This amounts effectively to placing ourselves in a frame of reference rotating at the Larmor frequency which in the present case is the same as the frequency of the applied field.

4.2 MAGNETIZATION

Having obtained the density matrix representing an ensemble of spins $\frac{1}{2}$ perturbed by coherent r.f. radiation at the Larmor frequency and no relaxation, we can calculate easily the expectation value of various physical quantities represented by operators in quantum mechanics. We shall limit ourselves to the components of magnetization. We shall calculate their expectation value from the relation we have derived earlier:

$$\overline{\langle M_i \rangle} = \text{Tr}\,(M_i\varrho) \quad i = x, y, z \tag{4.23}$$

The operator M_i is given by the relation:

$$M_i = \gamma \hbar I_i \qquad (4.24)$$

where for a spin $I = \frac{1}{2}$

$$I_x = \begin{pmatrix} 0 & \dfrac{1}{2} \\ \dfrac{1}{2} & 0 \end{pmatrix} \qquad I_y = \begin{pmatrix} 0 & -\dfrac{i}{2} \\ \dfrac{i}{2} & 0 \end{pmatrix} \qquad I_z = \begin{pmatrix} \dfrac{1}{2} & 0 \\ 0 & \dfrac{1}{2} \end{pmatrix} \qquad (4.25)$$

With the matrix (4.20) for ϱ, we obtain for N particles:

$$\overline{\langle M_z \rangle} = N \frac{\gamma \hbar}{2} \cos \omega_1 t \qquad (4.26)$$

For M_x, we get:

$$\overline{\langle M_x \rangle} = -N \frac{\gamma \hbar}{4} i \sin \omega_1 t \, [\exp (i\omega_0 t) - \exp (-i\omega_0 t)] \qquad (4.27)$$

$$= +N \frac{\gamma \hbar}{2} \sin \omega_1 t \sin \omega_0 t \qquad (4.28)$$

Similarly, we obtain:

$$\overline{\langle M_y \rangle} = +N \frac{\gamma \hbar}{2} \sin \omega_1 t \cos \omega_0 t \qquad (4.29)$$

We see that the r.f. field drives the spins in "unison", and produces in the xy plane, a magnetization oscillating at the Larmor frequency ω_0. The amplitude of the components of magnetization however are modulated at the frequency ω_1. This simply means that the magnetization vector M originally along the z axis is tilted towards the xy plane while it precesses around the z axis at the frequency ω_0. The net effect is thus clearly a precession of M around the direction of H_{rot}. We can also define:

$$\overline{\langle M_{xy} \rangle} = \overline{\langle M_x \rangle} + i \overline{\langle M_y \rangle} \qquad (4.30)$$

which can be written:

$$\overline{\langle M_{xy} \rangle} = + \frac{\gamma \hbar}{2} \sin \omega_1 t \, [\exp (i\omega_0 t)] \qquad (4.31)$$

reflecting the rotation of the projection of M in the xy plane at the frequency ω_0.

The whole phenomenon is called "magnetic resonance".

4*

If nothing else happens to our system, the components of the magnetization under the drive of the r.f. field will keep obeying the laws just obtained. However, interactions in our physical systems destroy the phase relationship between the individual spins. These interactions consequently tend to destroy the magnetization.

4.3 $\pi/2$ AND π PULSES

We have obtained the components of magnetization as:

$$\langle\overline{\overline{M_x}}\rangle = +N\frac{\gamma\hbar}{2}\sin\omega_1 t \sin\omega_0 t \tag{4.32}$$

$$\langle\overline{\overline{M_y}}\rangle = +N\frac{\gamma\hbar}{2}\sin\omega_1 t \cos\omega_0 t \tag{4.33}$$

$$\langle\overline{\overline{M_z}}\rangle = N\frac{\gamma\hbar}{2}\cos\omega_1 t \tag{4.34}$$

The angular frequency ω_1 reflects the strength of the applied r.f. field through the relation $\omega_1 = \gamma H_1$. The length of time of application of the field is entirely under the control of the experimentor; say H_1 is applied as a pulse for a time t_p. Then, we can define the driving phase angle of the pulse as:

$$\omega_1 t_p = \gamma H_1 t_p = \theta_p \tag{4.35}$$

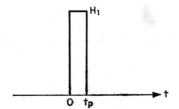

Figure 4.2   A r.f. pulse of length t_p

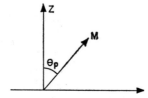

Figure 4.3   Tipping of the magnetization by a r.f. pulse

If $\theta_p = \pi/2$, we obtain:

$$\langle\overline{\overline{M_x}}\rangle = -N\frac{\gamma\hbar}{2}\sin\omega_0 t \tag{4.36}$$

$$\langle\overline{\overline{M_y}}\rangle = -N\frac{\gamma\hbar}{2}\cos\omega_0 t \tag{4.37}$$

$$\langle\overline{\overline{M_z}}\rangle = 0 \tag{4.38}$$

The magnetization is entirely tilted in the xy plane by such a pulse which, for obvious reasons is called a $\pi/2$ pulse. A π pulse is one which makes

$$M_x = M_y = 0 \quad \text{and} \quad M_z(t_p) = -M_z(0), \quad \theta_p = \pi$$

Of course, θ_p can take any values. We are only limited by field strength available in the laboratory since relaxation will not permit, as we shall see, pulses of arbitrary length of time. We should note also that those remarks apply similarly to the matrices (4.20) and (4.22); a $\pi/2$ pulse is one which makes the population difference equal to zero and the density matrix off-diagonal elements maximum.

4.4 RANDOM PERTURBATION FOR THE CASE $I = 1/2$

In the case we have a stationary random perturbation acting on the ensemble of spins, we can apply directly the results of section 4.3.

For the time variation of the elements, we obtain, keeping only secular terms for which $\alpha - \alpha' = \beta - \beta'$:

$$\left(\frac{d\varrho'_{11}}{dt}\right)_{\text{rel}} = R_{1111}\varrho'_{11} + R_{1122}\varrho'_{22} \tag{4.39}$$

$$\left(\frac{d\varrho'_{22}}{dt}\right)_{\text{rel}} = R_{2211}\varrho'_{11} + R_{2222}\varrho'_{22} \tag{4.40}$$

$$\left(\frac{d\varrho'_{12}}{dt}\right)_{\text{rel}} = R'_{1212}\varrho'_{12} \tag{4.41}$$

$$\left(\frac{d\varrho'_{21}}{dt}\right)_{\text{rel}} = R'_{2121}\varrho'_{21} \tag{4.42}$$

where $R_{\alpha\alpha'\beta\beta'}$ is given by equation (3.57) and the prime on $R'_{\alpha\alpha'\beta\beta'}$ indicates that it is complex. The respective values of $R_{\alpha\alpha'\beta\beta'}$ are:

$$R_{1111} = -\frac{1}{\hbar^2} J_{2121}(\omega_{21}) \tag{4.43}$$

with similar expressions for the other parameters. We assume for the present case that transitions from 1 to 2 have the same probability as from 2 to 1, and define W_1 as:

$$W_1 = \frac{1}{\hbar^2} J_{2121}(\omega_{21}) = \frac{1}{\hbar^2} J_{1212}(\omega_{12}) \tag{4.44}$$

In equation (4.42), the complex R'_{2121} may be written:

$$R'_{2121} = \frac{1}{\hbar^2} \left\{ \frac{1}{2} (2J_{2211}(0) - J_{2222}(0) - J_{1111}(0) \right.$$

$$- J_{1212}(\omega_{12}) - J_{2121}(\omega_{21})$$

$$+ i(2k_{2211}(0) - k_{2222}(0) - k_{1111}(0)$$

$$\left. - k_{1212}(\omega_{12}) - k_{2121}(\omega_{21}) \right\} \tag{4.45}$$

We write that simply as:

$$R'_{2121} = W_2 + i\alpha \tag{4.46}$$

In the present equations, it is observed that we have spectral densities at 0 frequencies, as well as spectral densities at the frequency ω_{12} which of course is the Larmor or resonance frequency of the spins. The interaction at zero frequency reflects, for example, the broadening of the levels that could be due to an applied magnetic field which is inhomogeneous in the z direction; in other words, the precession frequency of the spins is different for different groups of spins producing a loss of the relative phase between those spins and the r.f. field. The terms which appear at the spectral density ω_{21} reflect the transitions that could be produced by the random perturbation; this could be, for example, a magnetic field fluctuating randomly, or a field having inhomogeneities in the xy plane while the spins are moving randomly in space. Thus, the whole picture could be that of spins moving in an inhomogeneous field. We can thus write our rate equations as:

$$\frac{d\varrho'_{11}}{dt} = W_1(-\varrho'_{11} + \varrho'_{22}) \tag{4.47}$$

$$\frac{d\varrho'_{22}}{dt} = W_1(\varrho'_{11} - \varrho'_{22}) \tag{4.48}$$

$$\frac{d\varrho'_{21}}{dt} = W_2\varrho'_{21} - i\alpha\varrho'_{21} \tag{4.49}$$

We can now add those results to the results obtained in the case of a coherent perturbation with the rule:

$$\frac{d\varrho}{dt} = \left(\frac{d\varrho}{dt}\right)_{rel} + \left(\frac{d\varrho}{dt}\right)_{r.f.} \tag{4.50}$$

Taking into account that we have already taken care of $\mathscr{H}_0$ in equation (4.17), (4.18) and (4.19), we can transform directly equation (4.47) through (4.49) to the Schrödinger representation to obtain:

$$\frac{d\varrho_{11}}{dt} = W_1(-\varrho_{11} + \varrho_{22}) + \omega_1 \operatorname{Im} \varrho_{21} \exp(-i\omega t) \qquad (4.51)$$

$$\frac{d\varrho_{22}}{dt} = W_1(\varrho_{11} - \varrho_{22}) - \omega_1 \operatorname{Im} \varrho_{21} \exp(-i\omega t) \qquad (4.52)$$

$$\frac{d\varrho_{21}}{dt} = i\omega_0 \varrho_{21} - W_2 \varrho_{21} - i\varkappa\varrho_{21} - \frac{i\omega_1}{2} \exp(i\omega t)$$

$$\times \exp(i\omega t)(\varrho_{11} - \varrho_{22}) \qquad (4.53)$$

This is the set of equations we have to solve for various experimental situations. The reader familiar with Bloch's formalism in nuclear magnetic resonance will see a large ressemblance between those three equations and Bloch's equations.

4.5 BLOCH SUSCEPTIBILITIES

Equation (4.51) through (4.53) can be solved exactly relative to the ϱ's in the following way. Substracting (4.52) from (4.51), defining:

$$\varrho_{11} - \varrho_{22} = \varDelta \qquad (4.54)$$

and assuming that $\varDelta$ tends to an equilibrium value $\varDelta_B$ rather than zero in the absence of r.f. fields, we get:

$$\frac{d\varDelta}{dt} = -\gamma_1(\varDelta - \varDelta_B) + 2\omega_1 \operatorname{Im} \delta \qquad (4.55)$$

The value $\varDelta_B$ may be the Boltzman equilibrium value. We assume that our solution for the off-diagonal elements has the form:

$$\varrho_{21} = \delta\,[\exp(i\omega t)] \qquad (4.56)$$

which, when replaced in equation (4.53) gives:

$$\frac{d\delta}{dt} = i(\omega_0 - \omega - \alpha)\,\delta - \gamma_2\delta - \frac{i\omega_1}{2}\varDelta \qquad (4.57)$$

We have defined:

$$\gamma_1 = 2W_1 = \frac{1}{T_1} \tag{4.58}$$

$$\gamma_2 = W_2 = \frac{1}{T_2} \tag{4.59}$$

Equation (4.57) contains a term $(\omega_0 - \omega - \alpha)$ which can be written $(\omega' - \omega)$ where ω' is the new resonance frequency perturbed by the relaxation processes:

$$\omega_0 - \alpha = \omega' \tag{4.60}$$

The solution of equation (4.57) and (4.55) can be obtained by assuming a stationary state in which Δ and δ are constants. Thus we can make $d\Delta/dt$ and $d\delta/dt$ equal to zero. Since that method of solution will be used again, relative to maser theory described in a further section, we will do it in some detail. From equation (4.57) we obtain:

$$\delta = -\frac{i(\omega_1/2)\,\Delta}{\gamma_2 + i(\omega - \omega')} \tag{4.61}$$

$$\delta = -\frac{(\omega_1/2)\,\Delta(\omega - \omega')}{\gamma_2^2 + (\omega - \omega')^2} - i\,\frac{(\omega_1/2)\,\gamma_2\Delta}{\gamma_2^2 + (\omega - \omega')^2} \tag{4.62}$$

On the other hand replacing Im δ in equation (4.55) with $d\Delta/dt = 0$ we get:

$$\Delta = \frac{\gamma_1\Delta_B}{\gamma_1 + \dfrac{\omega_1^2\gamma_2}{\gamma_2^2 + (\omega - \omega')^2}} \tag{4.63}$$

which gives finally for δ and Δ:

$$\delta = -\frac{\Delta_B T_2}{2}\,\frac{\gamma H_1 T_2(\omega - \omega') + i\gamma H_1}{1 + (\omega - \omega')^2\,T_2^2 + \gamma^2 H_1^2 T_1 T_2} \tag{4.64}$$

$$\Delta = \Delta_B\frac{1 + (\omega - \omega')^2\,T_2^2}{1 + (\omega - \omega')^2\,T_2^2 + \gamma^2 H_1^2 T_1 T_2} \tag{4.65}$$

The expectation value of the components of the magnetization can be calculated through equation (4.23) to obtain:

$$\overline{\overline{\langle M_z \rangle}} = \frac{N\gamma\hbar}{2}(\varrho_{11} - \varrho_{22}) \tag{4.66}$$

$$\overline{\overline{\langle M_x \rangle}} = \frac{N\gamma\hbar}{2}(\varrho_{21} + \varrho_{12}) \tag{4.67}$$

We define:

$$\overline{\overline{\langle M_z \rangle}}_0 = M_0 = \frac{\gamma \hbar}{2} N \Delta_B \tag{4.68}$$

$$\chi_0 = \frac{M_0}{H_0} \tag{4.69}$$

Combining equation (4.64) through (4.69), we finally obtain:

$$\overline{\overline{\langle M_z \rangle}} = \chi_0 H_0 \frac{1 + (\omega - \omega')^2 T_2^2}{1 + (\omega - \omega')^2 T_2^2 + \gamma^2 H_1^2 T_1 T_2} \tag{4.70}$$

$$\overline{\overline{\langle M_x \rangle}} = \frac{1}{2} \chi_0 H_0 \gamma T_2 \frac{T_2(\omega' - \omega) 2H_1 \cos \omega t + 2H_1 \sin \omega t}{1 + (\omega - \omega')^2 T_2^2 + \gamma^2 H_1^2 T_1 T_2} \tag{4.71}$$

A similar expression is obtained for $\overline{\overline{\langle M_y \rangle}}$. The r.f. susceptibilities are defined as:

$$\chi = \chi' - i\chi'' \tag{4.72}$$

and

$$M_x = \chi' 2H_1 \cos \omega t + \chi'' 2H_1 \sin \omega t \tag{4.73}$$

which gives:

$$\chi' = \frac{1}{2} \chi_0 H_0 \gamma T_2 \frac{T_2(\omega' - \omega)}{1 + (\omega' - \omega)^2 T_2^2 + \gamma^2 H_1^2 T_1 T_2} \tag{4.74}$$

$$\chi'' = \frac{1}{2} \chi_0 H_0 \gamma T_2 \frac{1}{1 + (\omega' - \omega)^2 T_1^2 + \gamma^2 H_1^2 T_1 T_2} \tag{4.75}$$

which are well known as the Bloch susceptibilities. We have thus seen that our simple model of an ensemble of spin $I = 1/2$ perturbed by a random perturbation and a r.f. field at the same time, gives Bloch susceptibilities as our solution. However it should be mentioned that this is not a general

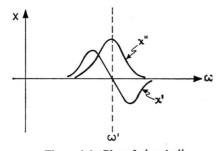

Figure 4.4 Plot of χ' and χ''

proof of that result. It works well for a spin $\frac{1}{2}$ perturbed by a random perturbation. Under the effect of the perturbation, the density matrix elements for the case $I = \frac{1}{2}$ relax exponentially with time towards their equilibrium value; this is a straightforward result of Redfield's theory. This is what gives the Lorentz shape of the r.f. susceptibility χ''. For a multi-level system, with unequal spacings, the spectral densities of the random perturbation may be different for different pairs of levels (different resonant frequencies) and the decay of the density matrix elements will not in general be exponential; the solution given by equation (4.70) and (4.71) for the magnetization components will not be valid in general.

4.6 π AND $\pi/2$ PULSES IN THE PRESENCE OF RELAXATION

The presence of relaxation in a system of spins affects the concept of π and $\pi/2$ pulses. However, since in normal experimental situations, the strength and length of the pulse are under control, it is possible still to define those pulses in relatively simple terms. Let us apply the r.f. field exactly at resonance with the spins. Further, for simplicity, we assume that the equilibrium of the populations among the energy levels is a uniform distribution when the r.f. field is absent. By this we mean that Δ, the difference of populations between the two levels, tends to zero at equilibrium in the absence of externally applied r.f. fields. Equation (4.55) and (4.57) can then be written:

$$\frac{d\Delta}{dt} = -\gamma_1 \Delta + 2\omega_1 \operatorname{Im} \delta \tag{4.76}$$

$$\frac{d\delta}{dt} = -\gamma_2 \delta - \frac{i\omega_1}{2} \Delta \tag{4.77}$$

The solution of these two equations is given by:

$$\delta = -\frac{i\Delta_0 \omega_1}{2S} \left[\exp\left(-1/2\right)(\gamma_1 + \gamma_2)\, t\right] \sin St \tag{4.78}$$

$$\Delta = \Delta_0 \left[\exp\left(-1/2\right)(\gamma_1 + \gamma_2)\, t\right] \left\{\cos St + \frac{(\gamma_2 - \gamma_1)}{2S} \sin St\right\} \tag{4.79}$$

The algebra necessary to obtain that result is somewhat involved and will not be given here. In these expressions, the symbol Δ_0 is the value of Δ at time $t = 0$. This finite difference of population can be obtained by various means like optical pumping, magnetic selection or other methods, as will be seen later. The symbol S stands for:

$$S = \sqrt{\omega_1^2 - \tfrac{1}{4}(\gamma_2 - \gamma_1)^2} \qquad (4.80)$$

Of course, equations (4.78) and (4.79) take a very simple form in the case:

$$\gamma_2 = \gamma_1 = \gamma$$

In that case, we have:

$$\delta = -\frac{i\Delta_0}{2} [\exp(-\gamma t) \sin \omega_1 t] \qquad (4.81)$$

$$\Delta = \Delta_0 [\exp(-\gamma t) \cos \omega_1 t] \qquad (4.82)$$

and π, $\pi/2$ pulses keep their meaning given in section 4.3 except that for a $\pi/2$ pulse the magnetization in the xy plane is not proportional to Δ_0 but rather to $\Delta_0 \exp(-\gamma t)$. However if the r.f. field available is relatively strong, or in other words if:

$$\gamma H_1 \gg \gamma_1, \gamma_2 \qquad (4.83)$$

then, for a $\pi/2$ or π pulse, the length of the pulse t_p may be made short enough so as to make relaxation negligible during that time. In that case, the results of section 4.3 apply entirely and the magnetization originally along z can be tipped entirely in the xy plane.

4.7 STIMULATED EMISSION

One may wonder what happens to the magnetization when it is tipped towards the xy plane. The question is best answered if we place ourselves in an environment such as a microwave cavity or a r.f. coil.

Instead of looking at the oscillating magnetization as such we will look rather at the quantum mechanical behaviour of that system in such a situation.

Let us assume that after the applied field is turned off, there exists in the cavity an r.f. field which, for instance, may be produced by the atoms themselves. From definition of electromagnetic parameters in a cavity we can write.

$$\text{Power dissipated in the cavity} = \frac{\omega W}{Q_l} \qquad (4.84)$$

where

$\omega \rightarrow$ frequency of the field

$W \rightarrow$ total energy in the cavity

$Q_l \rightarrow$ quality factor of the cavity

Those factors can be written explicitly to give:

$$P_{dis} = \frac{\omega}{8\pi Q_l} \int_{v_c} H_{rf}^2 \, dv \tag{4.85}$$

where v_c is the volume of the cavity and H_{rf} is the oscillating magnetic field. In the present calculation we may generalize somewhat by taking H_1 not constant over the volume occupied by the ensemble. We may have two extreme cases, where the atoms may either be assumed at rest, or free to move inside a container. The first case may be that of an ensemble of atoms diluted in a buffer gas at pressures of several Torr. Each atom then sees a field H_1 of its own. During the interaction time with H_1 ($\sim T_2$), they do not have time to move around much. This is a typical situation which is encountered in the rubidium maser, a device which will be studied later. The second case may be that of atoms contained in a storage bottle whose walls have been lined with a special coating; this coating prevents relaxation of the atoms upon collisions with the wall. The atoms are then free to move around until they hit the wall and then change direction abruptly. This random motion is rapid and the time of interaction with H_1 may be large compared to the time between two collisions; the atoms thus see the average of H_1.

Let us consider that last case. We define a filling factor η as

$$\eta = \frac{\langle H_1 \rangle_{v_a}^2}{\langle H_{rf}^2 \rangle_{v_c}} \tag{4.86}$$

where v_c is the cavity volume and v_a the volume occupied by the atoms. We also define $\langle \omega_1 \rangle$ as

$$\langle \omega_1 \rangle = \frac{1}{v_a} \int_{v_a} \gamma H_1 \, dv \tag{4.87}$$

and write

$$P_{dis} = \frac{\omega v_c}{8\pi Q \eta} \langle \omega_1 \rangle^2 \tag{4.88}$$

which gives the relation between the power dissipated in the cavity and a function of the field strength given by $H_1 = \omega_1/\gamma$. The power dissipated, however, must come from somewhere. The only source present after the r.f. pulse has been turned off is the atomic system itself.

The power emitted by the atoms is:

$P_{at} =$ (Energy quantum) $\times$ (Total number of atoms) $\times$ (Rate of transitions from upper level to lower level). This can be written:

$$P_{at} = -h\nu N_0 \left(\frac{d\varrho_{11}}{dt}\right)_{r.f.} \tag{4.89}$$

$$= -\frac{1}{2} h\nu N_0 \left(\frac{d\varDelta}{dt}\right)_{r.f.} \tag{4.90}$$

where $(d\varDelta/dt)_{r.f.}$ is the rate of change of $\varDelta$ due to the to r.f. field interaction and not the relaxation. We assume that this power is dissipated in the cavity and that at all times, P_{dis} equals P_{at}.

$$\langle\omega_1\rangle^2 = -\frac{8\pi Q_i\eta\mu_0^2 N_0}{2V_c\hbar}\left(\frac{d\varDelta}{dt}\right)_{r.f.} \tag{4.91}$$

Equation (4.91) gives the important relation between the field strength and the rate of change of the populations, due to an r.f. perturbation, in a self consistent approach. We thus end up with three equations describing the systems of spins in presence of a r.f. field which it produces itself. These are repeated here for convenience:

$$\frac{d\varDelta}{dt} = -\gamma_1\varDelta + 2\langle\omega_1\rangle \operatorname{Im} \delta \tag{4.92}$$

$$\frac{d\delta}{dt} = -\gamma_2\delta - \frac{i\langle\omega_1\rangle}{2}\varDelta \tag{4.93}$$

$$\left(\frac{d\varDelta}{dt}\right)_{r.f.} = -\frac{1}{k}\langle\omega_1\rangle^2 \tag{4.94}$$

where

$$\frac{1}{k} = \frac{2V_c\hbar}{8\pi Q_i\eta\mu_0^2 N_0} \tag{4.95}$$

There are two important cases which we would like to consider:

1) Case when the r.f. field is relatively weak.
Say for example that:

$$\langle\omega_1\rangle \ll \gamma_1, \gamma_2$$

In that case, the signal produced by the atoms is weak and does not perturb them as much as the relaxation which is present. Another way of seeing the problem is to say that the life time for induced radiation which is of the order of $1/\omega_1$ is long compared to the relaxation time T_1 and T_2. This permits us to neglect the terms in ω_1 in (4.92) and (4.93) and obtain:

$$\Delta = \Delta_0 \exp\left(-\gamma_1 t_1\right) \qquad (4.96)$$

$$\delta = \delta(\theta_p) \exp\left[-\gamma_2(t - t_1)\right] \qquad (4.97)$$

where t_1 is the time at which the r.f. pulse is applied after the creation of the unbalance Δ_0 in the populations. This population difference can be created by various means such as optical pumping, magnetic selection or

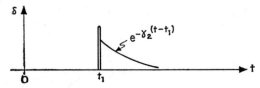

Figure 4.5　Decay of the amplitude of the density matrix off-diagonal elements after a r.f. pulse

others as mentioned earlier. From equation (4.94) and the radiative part of equation (4.92) we can write, taking into account that, at resonance, δ is imaginary, $(\delta = i\delta_i)$ (see equation (4.62)):

$$\left(\frac{d\Delta}{dt}\right)_{rad} = 2\langle\omega_1\rangle\,\delta_i = -\frac{1}{k}\langle\omega_1\rangle^2 \qquad (4.98)$$

which gives

$$\langle\omega_1\rangle = -2k\delta_i \qquad (4.99)$$

to finally obtain:

$$\left(\frac{d\Delta}{dt}\right)_{rad} = -4k\delta_i^2 \qquad (4.100)$$

and for the power radiated:

$$P = 2h\nu N_0 k\delta_i^2 \qquad (4.101)$$

$$= 2h\nu N_0 k\{\delta(\theta_p)\}^2 \exp\left[-2\gamma_2(t - t_1)\right] \qquad (4.102)$$

The power thus decays at twice the rate γ_2. The field however decays at the rate γ_2. From equation (4.99) we can write

$$H_1 = -\frac{2k}{\gamma}\,\delta(\theta_p) \exp\left[-\gamma_2(t - t_1)\right] \qquad (4.103)$$

With a linear detector the rate γ_2 is measured directly. For a pulse of phase angle $\pi/2$ we have:

$$|\delta|_{\pi/2} = \frac{\Delta}{2} \exp\left(-\gamma_1 t_1\right) \qquad (4.104)$$

since the amplitude of $|\delta|$ is necessarily proportional to the remaining population unbalance at time t_1. Consequently a plot of $|\delta|_{\pi/2}$ as a function of t_1, the time interval between the r.f. pulse and the time of creation of Δ_0, gives information on γ_1. That theory just described is fundamental in measurements of T_1 and T_2 by pulse technique.

2) Case where the r.f. field perturbation cannot be neglected relative to the relaxation.

In that case, we have to solve equation (4.92) and (4.93) in which $\omega_1 = \gamma H_1$ is not a constant but rather is given by equation (4.99). Replacing in equations (4.92) and (4.93) ω_1 given by that expression, we obtain:

$$\frac{d\Delta}{dt} = -4k\delta_i^2 - \gamma_1\Delta \tag{4.105}$$

$$\frac{d\delta}{dt} = k\delta_i\Delta - \gamma_2\delta_i \tag{4.106}$$

This set of equations cannot be solved as such. Some insight however about the actual behaviour of Δ and δ can be obtained by setting the relaxation rates equal to zero. In that case, we get an exact solution in terms of analytical functions.

Another case for which an exact analytical solution exists is the situation for which $\gamma_1 = \gamma_2 = \gamma$; it means that the off-diagonal elements relax at the same rate as the diagonal elements. In some masers, it is possible to satisfy this situation in some particular specific experimental situation. The solution can then be written as:

$$\delta_i = A \exp(-\gamma t) \operatorname{sech}(y + \varphi) \tag{4.107}$$

in which we have to find A, y and φ from the limiting conditions. We differentiate with respect to time, replace in equation (4.106), and equate members of sech to similar members, to obtain

$$k\Delta = -\tanh(y + \varphi)\frac{dy}{dt} \tag{4.108}$$

This last expression can be differentiated again and replaced in equation (4.105). Equating coefficients in front of sech terms, we finally obtain a particular solution implicit in the equation:

$$\frac{dy}{dt} = 2kA \exp(-\gamma t) \tag{4.109}$$

The solution for y and Δ is thus:

$$y = -\frac{2Ak}{\gamma} \exp(-\gamma t) + \text{constant} \tag{4.110}$$

$$\Delta = -2A \exp(-\gamma t) \tanh\left(-\frac{2Ak}{\gamma} \exp(-\gamma t) + \varphi\right) \tag{4.111}$$

where the constant is taken care of by the phase φ. To determine φ and A, we evaluate Δ at $t = 0$;

$$\Delta = -2A \tanh\left(\varphi - \frac{2Ak}{\gamma}\right) \tag{4.112}$$

We assume that the system has been prepared by a r.f. pulse of phase angle θ_p, at a time $t = 0$ at which a positive population unbalance Δ_0 existed. Thus, at the end of the pulse, if we assume the pulse length small compared to T_1 and T_2, we have:

$$\Delta = \Delta_0 \cos \theta_p \tag{4.113}$$

We then set:
$$2A = \Delta_0 \tag{4.114}$$

and

$$\tanh\left(\varphi - \frac{2Ak}{\gamma}\right) = \cos \theta_p \tag{4.115}$$

which implies:

$$\varphi = \frac{\Delta_0 k}{\gamma} - \ln\left(\tan \frac{\theta_p}{2}\right) \tag{4.116}$$

We finally obtain:

$$\Delta = \Delta_0 \exp(-\gamma t) \tanh\left(\frac{\Delta_0 k}{\gamma} \exp(-\gamma t) - \frac{\Delta_0 k}{\gamma} - \ln\left(\tan \frac{\theta_p}{2}\right)\right) \tag{4.117}$$

from which we get:

$$\delta = -\frac{i\Delta_0}{2} \exp(-\gamma t) \operatorname{sech}\left(-\frac{\Delta_0 k}{\gamma}(1 - \exp(-\gamma t)) - \ln\left(\tan \frac{\theta_p}{2}\right)\right)$$

$$\tag{4.118}$$

The power emitted by the atoms is:

$$\boxed{\begin{aligned} P_{at} &= \frac{1}{2} h\nu N_0 k \Delta_0^2 \exp(-2\gamma t) \\ &\times \operatorname{sech}^2\left(-\frac{\Delta_0 k}{\gamma}(1 - \exp(-\gamma t)) - \ln\left(\tan \frac{\theta_p}{2}\right)\right) \end{aligned}} \tag{4.119}$$

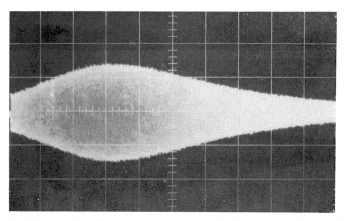

Figure 4.6 Power emitted by an atomic system with Δ_0 positive after a r.f. pulse of phase angle smaller than $\pi/2$.

There will be a maximum in emitted power when $dP/dt = 0$ or when the following equation is satisfied:

$$1 = \frac{\Delta_0 k}{\gamma} \exp\left(-\gamma\tau_M\right) \tanh\left(-\frac{\Delta_0 k}{\gamma}\left(1 - \exp\left(\gamma\tau_M\right)\right) - \ln\left(\tan\frac{\theta_p}{2}\right)\right)$$

(4.120)

where τ_M is the time at which the maximum appears. A plot of equation (4.119) for a given θ_p and k is given by figure 4.6.

The theory just developed is fundamental to maser theory. It shows that an ensemble of spins in the proper environment (cavity) having a positive population unbalance ($\Delta_0 = \varrho_{11} - \varrho_{22}$) may be triggered into oscillation by an r.f. pulse. When the factor $\Delta_0 k/\gamma$ is large enough, it is possible to obtain a true oscillator since from equation (4.119), power builds up to a given maximum value. If the population unbalance Δ_0 is replenished by some means, we obtain a continuous oscillation, hence a maser.

4.8 SPIN ECHO

We have just seen how stimulated emission signals can be obtained out of a macroscopic ensemble of spins after a pulse of phase angle θ. In particular we have introduced the concept of $\pi/2$ and π pulses. We would like now to study the situation in which two such pulses of phase angle θ are applied in succession.

We first divide our macroscopic ensemble into sub-ensembles whose density matrices are $\varrho_{\omega'}$. We assume that a non-homogeneous broadening exists in the sample. For example, a gradient of a magnetic field could exist creating a situation in which the various sub-ensembles $\varrho_{\omega'}$ have different resonant frequencies. That could be illustrated, for example, by various precession rates of the magnetization of such sub-ensembles in the xy plane. Second, we assume that the line width produced by other homogeneous processes which are present in the sample such as magnetic dipole interaction, is smaller than the line width produced by the inhomogeneous broadening. Finally we assume that we have an ensemble of spins $I = \frac{1}{2}$.

Equation (4.22) describes the density matrix of an ensemble of spins after a r.f. pulse of phase angle $\omega_1 t = \theta$ in the interaction representation. The original matrix at time $t = 0$ was one representing an ensemble completely polarized in which all elements were zero except ϱ_{11} which was unity. That matrix [equation (4.22)] was obtained from the solution of the differential equations (4.17), (4.18) and (4.19). We would like, however, for the present purpose, to use an operator formalism, which does not necessitate the solution of differential equations but rather requires only the multiplication of matrices. We actually want an operator $R(\theta)$ which when applied to $\varrho'_{\omega'}$ performs the operation of a r.f. pulse at the resonant frequency of the ensemble through the operator transformation:

$$\varrho'_{\omega'}(\theta) = R\varrho'_{\omega'}R^{-1} \tag{4.121}$$

The evolution in time of $\varrho'_{\omega'}(\theta)$ can then be computed from relation (2.80), repeated here:

$$\varrho(t) = \exp\left[-(i/\hbar)\,\mathscr{H}_0 t\right]\varrho(0)\exp\left[(i/\hbar)\,\mathscr{H}_0 t\right] \tag{4.122}$$

The operator R is a matrix which has the same order as $\varrho'_{\omega'}$. In the case of $I = \frac{1}{2}$ we may write for a pulse whose magnetic field vector is along the x axis:

$$R(\theta, x) = \begin{pmatrix} \cos\theta/2 & i\sin\theta/2 \\ i\sin\theta/2 & \cos\theta/2 \end{pmatrix} \tag{4.123a}$$

If the oscillating magnetic field is along the y axis, we have:

$$R(\theta, y) = \begin{pmatrix} \cos\theta/2 & -\sin\theta/2 \\ \sin\theta/2 & \cos\theta/2 \end{pmatrix} \tag{4.123b}$$

Matrix (4.123b) may be recognized as a representation of the full rotation group $D^{(1/2)}$ with the other Euler angles φ and Ψ both equal to zero. The elements of $R(\theta, x)$ on the other hand are the Cailey-Klein parameters with φ and Ψ equal to zero.

Either of the two matrices can be used for the present problem. Earlier in the present chapter we have used the magnetic field vector along x. To be consistent with that notation we would have to use the transformation $R(\theta, x)$. However one gains in setting the magnetic field vector along y since it permits the use of the full rotation groups in more complex problems where $I > \frac{1}{2}$, groups which are well known and tabulated. For that reason we shall use $H_{r.f.}$ along the y axis.

We apply $D^{1/2}(\varphi, \theta, \Psi) = D^{1/2}(0, \theta, 0)$ on a matrix representing a sample completly polarized:

$$\varrho'_{\omega'} = \begin{pmatrix} 1 & 0 \\ 0 & 0 \end{pmatrix} \tag{4.124}$$

The matrix obtained is in the laboratory frame of reference:

$$\varrho_{\omega'}(\theta, t) = \begin{pmatrix} \cos^2 \theta/2 & \frac{1}{2} \sin \theta \exp (i\omega't) \\ \frac{1}{2} \sin \theta \exp (-i\omega't) & \sin^2 \theta/2 \end{pmatrix} \tag{4.125}$$

Relation (4.125) represents a sub-ensemble which has a resonant frequency ω', different from ω_0, the mean for the whole ensemble, by the amount $\Delta\omega$. In the interaction representation in which the frame of reference rotates at the mean Larmor frequency ω_0 that subensemble appears to precess at a rate $\Delta\omega$ where the sign is given by the difference $(\omega' - \omega_0)$:

$$\Delta\omega = \omega' - \omega_0 \tag{4.126}$$

We assume that the distribution of $\Delta\omega$ is given by a gaussian representation such as:

$$g(\Delta\omega) = (2\pi\sigma^2)^{-1/2} \exp [-(\Delta\omega)^2/2\sigma^2] \tag{4.127}$$

The factor σ represents the r.m.s. deviation in precessional frequency from the mean ω_0 due to the applied gradient.

We are interested in the magnetization in the xy plane which may induce observable signals in coils or cavities surrounding the ensemble. We thus calculate the average value of I_y given by:

$$\langle I_y \rangle_{\omega'av} = \text{Tr}\,(I_y\varrho) \tag{4.128}$$

That gives:

$$\langle I_y \rangle_{\omega'av} = \frac{i}{4} \sin \theta\, [\exp (i\omega't) - \exp (-i\omega't)] \tag{4.129}$$

The average value of $\langle I_y \rangle_{\omega'}$ over all possible values of ω' in the ensemble is given by:

$$\overline{\overline{\langle I_y \rangle}} = - \int\limits_{-\infty}^{+\infty} (2\pi\sigma^2)^{-1/2} \exp [-(\Delta\omega)^2/2\sigma^2]$$

$$\left\{\frac{1}{4i} \sin \theta\, [\exp [i(\Delta\omega + \omega_0)\, t] - \exp [-i(\Delta\omega + \omega_0)\, t]]\right\} d(\Delta\omega) \tag{4.130}$$

This last equation is easily integrated to give:

$$\overline{\overline{\langle I_y \rangle}} = \tfrac{1}{2} \sin \theta \sin \omega_0 t \exp (-t^2\sigma^2/2) \tag{4.131}$$

This is the law which describes the decay of the Y component of the whole ensemble angular momentum for a gaussian distribution of resonant fre-

5*

quencies. Had we used a Lorentz distribution we would have obtained a simple exponential decay.

We would like now to study the case when another pulse of the same phase angle θ is applied at a time $t = \tau$ later. For mathematical simplicity, we restrict ourselves, here, to a pulse of the same phase angle than the first one; however, we still obtain essentially the results we are looking for.

At time $t = \tau$ in the interaction representation, relation (4.125) can be written:

$$\varrho'_{\omega'}(\theta, \tau) = \begin{pmatrix} \cos^2 \theta/2 & \tfrac{1}{2} \sin \theta \exp (i\Delta\omega\tau) \\ \tfrac{1}{2} \sin \theta \exp (-i\Delta\omega\tau) & \sin^2 \theta/2 \end{pmatrix} \tag{4.132}$$

We apply to that $\varrho'_{\omega'}(\theta, \tau)$ the operator $R(\theta)$ which corresponds to applying another pulse to the sub-ensemble ω'. The matrix obtained (not simplified) has the form given on page 69. We calculate $\langle I_y \rangle_{\omega'av}$ from equation (4.128) and obtain in the laboratory frame:

$$\langle I_y \rangle_{\omega'av} = -\frac{i}{2} \left\{ \cos^3 \frac{\theta}{2} \sin \frac{\theta}{2} + \frac{1}{2} \sin \theta \cos^2 \frac{\theta}{2} \exp (i\omega'\tau) \right.$$

$$\left. - \frac{1}{2} \sin \theta \sin^2 \frac{\theta}{2} \exp (-i\omega'\tau) - \sin^3 \frac{\theta}{2} \cos \frac{\theta}{2} \right\} \exp (i\omega't)$$

$$+ \frac{i}{2} \left\{ \cos^3 \frac{\theta}{2} \sin \frac{\theta}{2} - \frac{1}{2} \sin \theta \sin^2 \frac{\theta}{2} \exp (i\omega'\tau) \right.$$

$$\left. + \frac{1}{2} \sin \theta \cos^2 \frac{\theta}{2} \exp (-i\omega'\tau) - \cos \frac{\theta}{2} \sin^3 \frac{\theta}{2} \right\} \exp (-i\omega't') \tag{4.133}$$

where t' is measured from time τ, and the pulse lenght is assumed negligible relative to τ. We now average over all values of ω' in the same way as we did earlier, to obtain:

$$\overline{\langle I_y \rangle} = \frac{1}{2} \left\{ \sin \theta \cos \theta \sin \omega_0 t' \exp (-t'^2\sigma^2/2) \right.$$

$$+ \sin \theta \cos^2 \frac{\theta}{2} \sin \omega_0(t'+ \tau) \exp [-(\tau + t')^2 \sigma^2/2]$$

$$\left. + \sin \theta \sin^2 \frac{\theta}{2} \sin \omega_0(t' + \tau) \exp [-(\tau - t')^2 \sigma^2/2] \right\} \tag{4.134}$$

$$(R\varrho'R^{-1}) = \begin{bmatrix} \cos^4\dfrac{\theta}{2} - \dfrac{1}{2}\sin\theta\sin\dfrac{\theta}{2}\cos\dfrac{\theta}{2}\exp(i\,\Delta\omega\tau) - \dfrac{1}{2}\sin\theta\sin\dfrac{\theta}{2}\cos\dfrac{\theta}{2}\exp(-i\,\Delta\omega\tau) + \sin^4\dfrac{\theta}{2} & \cos^3\dfrac{\theta}{2}\sin\dfrac{\theta}{2} + \dfrac{1}{2}\sin\theta\cos^2\dfrac{\theta}{2}\exp(i\,\Delta\omega\tau) - \dfrac{1}{2}\sin\theta\sin^2\dfrac{\theta}{2}\exp(-i\,\Delta\omega\tau) - \sin^3\dfrac{\theta}{2}\cos\dfrac{\theta}{2} \\[2em] \cos^3\dfrac{\theta}{2}\sin\dfrac{\theta}{2} - \dfrac{1}{2}\sin\theta\sin^2\dfrac{\theta}{2}\exp(i\,\Delta\omega\tau) + \dfrac{1}{2}\sin\theta\cos^2\dfrac{\theta}{2}\exp(-i\,\Delta\omega\tau) - \sin^3\dfrac{\theta}{2}\cos\dfrac{\theta}{2} & \cos^2\dfrac{\theta}{2}\sin^2\dfrac{\theta}{2} + \dfrac{1}{2}\sin\theta\sin\dfrac{\theta}{2}\cos\dfrac{\theta}{2}\exp(i\,\Delta\omega\tau) + \dfrac{1}{2}\sin\theta\sin\dfrac{\theta}{2}\cos\dfrac{\theta}{2}\exp(-i\,\Delta\omega\tau) + \sin^2\dfrac{\theta}{2}\cos^2\dfrac{\theta}{2} \end{bmatrix}$$

The sequence of pulses is as on figure 4.7:

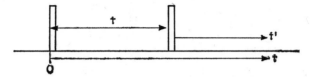

Figure 4.7   Sequence of r.f. pulses to obtain spin echoes

We may transform to t as measured from time 0 to obtain:

$$\overline{\overline{\langle I_y \rangle}} = \frac{1}{2} \left\{ \sin \theta \cos^2 \frac{\theta}{2} \sin \omega_0 t \exp \left[-(t^2 \sigma^2)/2 \right] \right.$$

$$+ \sin \theta \cos \theta \sin \omega_0 (t - \tau) \exp \left[-(t - \tau)^2 \sigma^2/2 \right]$$

$$\left. - \frac{1}{2} \sin \theta \sin^2 \frac{\theta}{2} \sin \omega_0 (t - 2\tau) \exp \left[-(t - 2\tau)^2 \sigma^2/2 \right] \right\} \qquad (4.135)$$

The magnetization and the signal induced in a coil enclosing the ensemble can then be obtained in a straightforward manner.

In that last equation, the first term represents the tail of the first induced signal; normally that signal dies out before the time at which the second pulse is applied. The second term gives the form of the induced signal after the second pulse. It dies out at the same rate as the signal after the first pulse. Finally the third term shows the presence of a signal at a time $t = 2\tau$ or at a time τ after the second pulse. That signal has a bell shape and is the so-called spin echo.

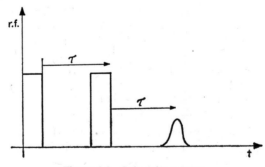

Figure 4.8   Spin echo pattern

CHAPTER 5

Selected Applications of the Density Matrix Formalism

IN THE PRECEDING section we have used our formalism to explain phenomena observed in the subject of magnetic resonance. It was shown quite clearly that the density matrix formalism is a very powerful tool in solving problems concerning ensemble of particles.

We would like now to apply our formalism to very specific problems like those encountered in the development of theories basic to devices like masers and lasers. This present section is thus really aimed at giving the theories basic to quantum electronics devices. We will study, here, subjects as, optical pumping, spin exchange interactions, microwave masers, optical lasers. In no cases we shall cover the subjects in all details; we shall only give the basic ideas and mathematics which will permit further reading on the subjects. Most of the calculations made are excerpts from recently published articles and the reader wishing to have more complete analyses is referred to the original articles listed in the bibliography.

5.1 OPTICAL PUMPING

Calculations of the interaction of resonance radiation with an ensemble of atoms make clear, in general, the appearance of three major effects. These are redistribution of populations among the sub-levels of the ground states of the atoms, displacement of the levels, an effect commonly called the "light shift", and destruction of the coherence that may exist in the ensemble of atoms in the ground state. A theory that leads to those results consists essentially in solving Schrödinger's equation in the context of standard perturbation theory; the coefficients of the wave function expanded into eigenvectors are calculated and the density matrix of the ensemble in the ground state is formed of the products of those coefficients.

An essential point in the theory is the representation of the source of radiation by an ideal model which approaches reality as much as possible.

One model consists in representing the radiation incident on the atoms as a large number N of plane waves with wave vectors k_i all parallel, and with the electrical vectors parallel to the unit vector e_λ. In that model, it is also assumed that the number of plane waves is very large; the wave vectors k_i are distributed around a mean value k_0 with a given law probability and a given bandwidth.

In the present theory we use for the radiation field a similar model, except that we want to consider the interaction of the radiation with the atoms as a stationary random perturbation. We assume that the radiation field is made of plane waves which interact with each atom on an individual basis; there is no coherence in the excitation of the atoms by the radiation field emitted by the light source. We assume, in other words, that when an atom absorbs or scatters a photon, the phase relationship that may exist at the site of another atom is destroyed; in this sense, we can say that the matrix elements representing the interaction between the field and the various atoms have no phase relationship. The atoms are perturbed in an incoherent way. This, of course, is very different from optical excitation such as that produced by a laser. In that case, the radiation beam shows a unique well determined phase and can drive the atoms "in unison".

We apply boldly the results of chapter 3 to a three level system which is submitted to resonance light that excites transitions between the levels as in figure 5.1:

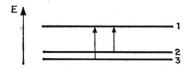

Figure 5.1   Simple three level system

We obtain three equations of the following form for the diagonal elements:

$$\frac{d\varrho'_{11}}{dt} = \frac{1}{\hbar^2} \{ J_{2121}(\omega_{21}) \varrho'_{22} + J_{3131}(\omega_{31}) \varrho'_{33}$$
$$- J_{1212}(\omega_{21}) \varrho'_{11} - J_{1313}(\omega_{31}) \varrho'_{11} \} \qquad (5.1)$$

$$\frac{d\varrho'_{22}}{dt} = \frac{1}{\hbar^2} \{ J_{1212}(\omega_{12}) \varrho'_{11} - J_{2121}(\omega_{12}) \varrho'_{22} \} \qquad (5.2)$$

$$\frac{d\varrho'_{33}}{dt} = \frac{1}{\hbar^2} \{ J_{1313}(\omega_{13}) \varrho'_{11} - J_{3131}(\omega_{13}) \varrho'_{33} \} \qquad (5.3)$$

In those expressions, the J's are taken as representing the spectral density of the light incident on the system. We must also consider, however, the effect of spontaneous emission. Since the lifetime for that last process is very short relative to the lifetime associated with the effect of the incident light, we may claim that there is no accumulation in level (1); furthermore, there is a balance between atoms coming in that level and those coming out of that level. We assume that the rate for spontaneous emission is equal for transitions towards both lower levels (2) and (3), a non-degenerate case, and we write:

$$\frac{d\varrho'_{11}}{dt} = 0 \tag{5.4}$$

which gives the possibility of writing:

$$\frac{d\varrho'_{22}}{dt} = \frac{1}{2\hbar^2}\{J_{3131}\varrho'_{33} - J_{2121}\varrho'_{22}\} \tag{5.5}$$

$$\frac{d\varrho'_{33}}{dt} = \frac{1}{2\hbar^2}\{J_{2121}\varrho'_{22} - J_{3131}\varrho'_{33}\} \tag{5.6}$$

For the off-diagonal element, we obtain:

$$\frac{d\varrho'_{23}}{dt} = -\frac{1}{\hbar^2}\{j_{3131}(\omega_{31}) + j_{1212}(\omega_{12})\}\varrho'_{23} \tag{5.7}$$

where $j_{3131}(\omega_{31})$ is given by equation (3.58), where specific members are in the present case:

$$J_{3131}(\omega_{31}) = \int_{-\infty}^{+\infty} G_{3131}(\tau)\,[\exp\,(-i\omega_{31}\tau)]\,d\tau \tag{5.8}$$

$$k_{3131}(\omega_{31}) = \int_{0}^{\infty} G_{3131}(\tau)\sin\omega_{31}\tau\,d\tau \tag{5.9}$$

Similar expressions can be written for the other member $j_{1212}(\omega_{12})$.

The imaginary term which appear in the rate equation describing the time variation of the off-diagonal elements ϱ'_{23} gives effectively a shift in the levels of the ground state. It is called the light shift.

In order to obtain tractable expressions for those two parameters we need to know the correlation function:

$$G_{3131}(\tau) = \overline{\langle 3 | \mathscr{H}_I(t) | 1 \rangle \langle 1 | \mathscr{H}_I(t + \tau) | 3 \rangle} \tag{5.10}$$

The perturbation from the radiation is, in its general form:*

$$\mathscr{H}_I = \frac{e}{mc} \mathbf{A} \cdot \mathbf{p} \tag{5.11}$$

where $\mathbf{A}$ is the potential vector and $\mathbf{p}$ is the generalized momentum. We take a special case where the light spectrum is filtered and has an appreciable spectral density only around the particular transition ω_{31}. That corresponds closely to the case of optical pumping in rubidium when isotopic filtering is used such as in the case of the rubidium maser.

In standard perturbation theory one normally writes $\mathbf{A}$ as a wave with a spatial and temporal dependence. In our model we assume the wave length to be long compared to the size of the atoms and write the interaction hamiltonian $\mathscr{H}$ as:

$$\langle 3 | \mathscr{H} | 1 \rangle = \frac{eA_0}{mc} \langle 3 | \boldsymbol{\varepsilon} \cdot \mathbf{p} | 1 \rangle f(t) \cos (\mathbf{k} \cdot \mathbf{v} - \omega) t \tag{5.12}$$

where $A_0 \boldsymbol{\varepsilon} \cos (\mathbf{k} \cdot \mathbf{v} - \omega) t$ represents a wave of frequency ω as seen by an atom moving at velocity v; $f(t)$ is a random modulation of the perturbation which explains the fact that the life time of the atoms in the excited state, limits the length of interaction with the incident wave. The correlation function of this perturbation is, assuming that the frequency ω is much larger than $1/\tau_0$, the inverse of the lifetime of the atoms in the excited state:

$$G(\tau) = \frac{1}{2} \overline{f(t) f(t + \tau)} \left(\frac{eA_0}{mc} \right)^2$$

$$\times \; |\langle 3 | \boldsymbol{\varepsilon} \cdot \mathbf{p} | 1 \rangle|^2 \cos (\mathbf{k} \cdot \mathbf{v}_1 - \omega_0) \tau \tag{5.13}$$

If we assume that $f(t)$ is a function passing from 0 to 1 randomly in time we finally obtain:

$$G(\tau) = \frac{1}{2} \left(\frac{eA_0}{mc} \right)^2 |\langle 3 | \boldsymbol{\varepsilon} \cdot \mathbf{p} | 1 \rangle|^2$$

$$\times \; \cos (\mathbf{k} \cdot \mathbf{v} - \omega_0) \tau \exp (- |\tau|/t_0) \tag{5.14}$$

---

* See for example L. I. Schiff, *Quantum Mechanics*, 3rd Edition.

where τ_0 is defined loosely as the correlation time and in fact is the life-time of the atom in the excited state. That correlation function has the form:

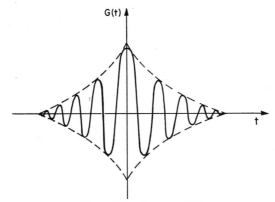

Figure 5.2   Form of $G(\tau)$

$G(\tau)$ is real as it should, since it represents an actual physical phenomenon. The J and K terms are then easily calculated as:

$$J_{3131}(\omega_{31}) = \frac{1}{2}\left(\frac{eA_0}{mc}\right)^2 |\langle 3| \, \boldsymbol{\varepsilon} \cdot \mathbf{p} \, |1\rangle|^2$$
$$\big|_{\substack{|\omega| \\ v_1}}$$

$$\times \frac{2\tau_0}{1 + (\mathbf{k} \cdot \mathbf{v}_1 - \omega + \omega_{31})^2 \, \tau_0^2} \qquad (5.15)$$

$$k_{3131}(\omega_{31}) = -\frac{1}{2}\left(\frac{eA_0}{mc}\right)^2 |\langle 3| \, \boldsymbol{\varepsilon} \cdot \mathbf{p} \, |1\rangle|^2$$
$$\big|_{\substack{|\omega| \\ v_1}}$$

$$\times \frac{(\mathbf{k} \cdot \mathbf{v}_1 - \omega + \omega_{31}) \, \tau_0^2}{1 + (\mathbf{k} \cdot \mathbf{v}_1 - \omega + \omega_{31})^2 \, \tau_0^2} \qquad (5.16)$$

Those expressions have to be integrated over all frequencies ω of the incident radiation which we assume has a spectrum $u(\omega)$. We then obtain:

$$J_{3131}(\omega_{31}) = \frac{1}{2}\left(\frac{eA_0}{mc}\right)^2 |\langle 3| \, \boldsymbol{\varepsilon} \cdot \mathbf{p} \, |1\rangle|^2$$
$$\big|_{v_1}$$

$$\int_{-\infty}^{+\infty} u(\omega) \frac{2\tau_0}{1 + (\mathbf{k} \cdot \mathbf{v} - \omega + \omega_{31})^2 \, \tau_0^2} \, d\omega \qquad (5.17)$$

$$k_{3131}(\omega_{31}) = -\frac{1}{2}\left(\frac{eA_0}{mc}\right)^2 |\langle 3| \, \boldsymbol{\varepsilon} \cdot \mathbf{p} \, |1\rangle|^2$$

$$\int_{-\infty}^{+\infty} u(\omega) \frac{(\mathbf{k} \cdot \mathbf{v}_1 - \omega + \omega_{31}) \tau_0^2}{1 + (\mathbf{k} \cdot \mathbf{v} - \omega + \omega_{31})^2 \tau_0^2} \tag{5.18}$$

That last expression shows that the light shift is absent if the center frequency of $u(\omega)$, assumed symmetrical, coïncides with the frequency $(\omega_{31} + \mathbf{k} \cdot \mathbf{v}_1)$ which is the resonating frequency of the atom. For all atoms, having a distribution of velocity, the actual average frequency shift depends on the symmetry of the distribution. Furthermore, if the center of both distributions, light spectrum and velocities do not coïncide, a shift in the energy levels exists.

    The results just obtained are similar to those obtained by Barrat and Cohen-Tannoudji in a different mathematical context. Those results can be put in a more general form. We define:

$$\frac{J_{\alpha e\alpha e}}{\hbar^2} = \Gamma_{\alpha e} \tag{5.19}$$

$$\frac{k_{\alpha e\alpha e}}{\hbar^2} = \delta_{\alpha e}^l \tag{5.20}$$

where $\Gamma_{\alpha e}$ is a pumping rate and $\delta_{\alpha e}^l$ is the light shift (not to be mixed with the amplitude of the off-diagonal matrix elements, notation used before). Then, we can write:

$$\frac{d\varrho'_{\alpha\alpha}}{dt} = -\Gamma_{\alpha e}\varrho'_{\alpha\alpha} \tag{5.21}$$

showing that the light tends to depopulate level α. Of course, one has to be careful in applying equation (5.21) since we have to take care of the polarization of the incident light. De-excitation of the upper state, which refills the bottom states, is not included in equation (5.21). This process has to be taken care of separately, by considering actual rates of spontaneous emission from the excited states. If e means the excited states then we have:

$$\frac{d\varrho'_{ee}}{dt} = \sum_{\alpha'} \Gamma_\alpha \varrho'_{\alpha\alpha'} - \sum_\alpha \gamma_{e\alpha}\varrho'_{ee} \tag{5.22}$$

$$\frac{d\varrho'_{\alpha\alpha}}{dt} = -\Gamma_\alpha \varrho'_{\alpha\alpha} + \gamma_{e\alpha}\varrho'_{ee} \tag{5.23}$$

where $\gamma_{e\alpha}$ is the rate of spontaneous emission from state e to state α. There is a special case where those equations are much simplified; that is the case when the atoms are de-excited by collisions with a buffer gas with equal probability to go to any of the ground states. Then equation (5.23) can be written as:

$$\frac{d\varrho'_{\alpha\alpha}}{dt} = -\Gamma_{\alpha}\varrho'_{\alpha\alpha} + \frac{\sum_{\alpha'} \Gamma_{\alpha'}}{N} \varrho'_{\alpha'\alpha'} \tag{5.24}$$

where N is the number of levels in the ground state. The effect of the light on the off-diagonal elements is calculated similarly as:

$$\frac{d\varrho_{\alpha\alpha'}}{dt} = -\frac{1}{\hbar^2} \{ j_{\alpha e\alpha e} + j_{e\alpha'e\alpha'} \} \varrho'_{\alpha\alpha'} \tag{5.25}$$

$$= -\frac{1}{\hbar^2} \left\{ \left(\frac{1}{2} J_{\alpha e\alpha e} + ik_{\alpha e\alpha e} \right) + \left(\frac{1}{2} J_{\alpha'e\alpha'e} - ik_{\alpha'e\alpha'e} \right) \right\} \varrho'_{\alpha\alpha'} \tag{5.26}$$

$$\boxed{\frac{d\varrho_{\alpha\alpha'}}{dt} = -\left\{ \left(\frac{\Gamma_\alpha}{2} + i\delta^e_\alpha \right) + \left(\frac{\Gamma_{\alpha'}}{2} - i\delta^e_{\alpha'} \right) \right\} \varrho'_{\alpha\alpha'}} \tag{5.27}$$

That expression assumes, of course, that the process of spontaneous emission returning atoms to the ground states destroy completly the phase relationship between that atom and the rest of the ensemble. There is thus, no phase memory in the present process after the optical pumping cycle.

Those equations are general and, consequently, can be applied to many cases to obtain the rate equations governing the dynamic behaviour of an ensemble of atoms interacting with radiation of the type given by most common lamps (not lasers). Other perturbations such as r.f. coherent radiation and relaxation can be added directly to those equations.

5.2 SPIN EXCHANGE INTERACTION

The importance of spin exchange interactions appears specially in the study of atomic oscillators, magnetic resonance in alkali vapours and other related subjects. In order to illustrate the effect of spin exchange on the behaviour of an ensemble of particles, we shall study in some detail the case of hydrogen.*

---

* In this section we shall follow the main lines of the theories developed by J. P. Wittke, Ph. D. Thesis Princeton, 1955, and P. L. Bender, *Phys. Rev.* **132** 2154, 1964.

The hydrogen atom is the most simple atomic structure: one electron and one proton interacting with each other electrostatically and magnetically. The electrostatic interaction gives the atom an energy level structure with a term $^2S_{1/2}$ lowest. The multiplicity is two, showing the presence of an electronic spin $\frac{1}{2}$; the orbital angular momentum is zero. Magnetic interaction between the proton and the electron spins produces two states with total angular momentum quantum numbers $F = 1$ and $F = 0$. The remaining degeneracy may be removed by an external magnetic field. That manifold of 4 states is 10 eV lower than the next highest terms $2S$ or $2P$. We shall thus consider that term alone assuming for the present, no connection between it and the higher ones.

Upon collision exchange of electrons may take place between two such atoms in their ground states and it is that problem that we actually want to consider. We want to obtain expressions for the relaxation times T_1 and T_2 and for the shift that may appear between the levels of the ground state manifold.

Hydrogen molecule

Suppose we take two hydrogen atoms and designate electron (1) on nucleus a and electron (2) on nucleus b. Let us call the wave functions orbital part respectively $u_a(1)$ and $u_b(2)$. The wave function of the ensemble of the two atoms is:

$$\psi = u_a(1)\, u_b(2) \tag{5.28}$$

However when the two atoms get close enough say at a distance r at which the electric fields of the electrons start to influence each other, it is not possible to tell which electron is which, and a wave function as good as the one given above may be:

$$\mathscr{E}\psi = u_a(2)\, u_b(1) \tag{5.29}$$

where E is the exchange operator.

The orbital wave function of the ensemble can then be written:

$$\psi = \frac{1}{2(1 \pm \alpha^2)}\left(u_a(1)\, u_b(2) \pm u_b(1)\, u_a(2)\right) \tag{5.30}$$

where α stands for the integral $\int u_a(1)\, u_b(1)\, d\tau_1$.

The minus sign gives an antisymmetric orbital while the plus sign gives the symmetric orbital.

The energy of the "molecule" is:

$$E_\pm = \frac{\langle ab| \mathscr{H} |ab\rangle \pm \langle ab| \mathscr{H} |ba\rangle}{1 \pm \alpha^2} \qquad (5.31)$$

where $\mathscr{H}$ is the hamiltonian taking into account kinetic energy terms and electrostatic potential energy.

The term $\langle ab| \mathscr{H} |ba\rangle$ is called the exchange integral and the energy has the well known shape shown in figure 5.3.

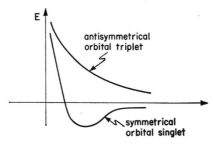

Figure 5.3   Energy of hydrogen molecule. The horizontal axis (r) is the internuclear distance

This model says that the electrons tend to cluster between the nuclei to have minimum energy and form a stable molecule. The introduction of electronic and nuclear spins in the picture is straightforward. Let us call the spin wave function $F_K(1, 2)$ in which K determines the hyperfine state for the case of the two coupled atoms; there are 16 such states. The wave function considering spins can thus be written:

$$\psi_K = u_a(1) u_b(2) F_K(1,2) \qquad (5.32)$$

An equally valid solution is for the two electrons exchanged physically:

$$E\psi_K = u_a(2) u_b(1) F_K(2,1) \qquad (5.33)$$

Since the total wave function must be antisymmetrical, we can write:

$$\Psi = (\psi_K - \mathscr{E}\psi_K)N \qquad (5.34)$$

where N is the normalizing constant. In case the atoms are kept far enough, we may write $N = 1/\sqrt{2}$. That wave functions is antisymmetrical. If we apply the operator exchange E to Ψ, the sign changes as it should. We define:

$$u_s = \frac{1}{\sqrt{2}} [u_a(1) u_b(2) + u_a(2) u_b(1)] \tag{5.35}$$

$$u_a = \frac{1}{\sqrt{2}} [u_a(1) u_b(2) - u_a(2) u_b(1)] \tag{5.36}$$

with the property:

$$\mathscr{E} u_s = u_s \tag{5.37}$$

$$\mathscr{E} u_a = -u_a \tag{5.38}$$

This permits us to write Ψ as:

$$\Psi_K = \tfrac{1}{2}[u_s(F_K - \mathscr{E} F_K) + u_a(F_K + \mathscr{E} F_K)] \tag{5.39}$$

When two atoms start from infinity and enter into collision, there is equal probability for atoms to form symmetrical or antisymmetrical orbitals. In equation (1.3) of chapter 1, the interaction hamiltonian $\mathscr{H}_0$ is not constant but is applied for a given time such that after the collision we obtain:

$$u_s^f = u_s \exp\left[-i \int_0^\tau (E_s/\hbar)\, dt\right] \tag{5.40}$$

$$u_a^f = u_a \exp\left[-i \int_0^\tau (E_a/\hbar)\, dt\right] \tag{5.41}$$

where τ is the time of duration of the collision. Let us define:

$$\int_0^\tau \frac{E_s}{\hbar}\, dt = \Delta_s \quad \text{(singlet)} \tag{5.42}$$

$$\int_0^\tau \frac{E_a}{\hbar}\, dt = \Delta_t \quad \text{(triplet)} \tag{5.43}$$

$$\Delta = \Delta_t - \Delta_s \tag{5.44}$$

We can thus write the total wave function after the collision as:

$$\Psi' = \tfrac{1}{2}[u_s(F_k - \mathscr{E} F_k) + u_a(F_k + \mathscr{E} F_k) \exp(-i\Delta)] \tag{5.45}$$

in which we have neglected an overall constant phase factor which has no physical meaning.

We see at once that if $\Delta = \pi$, we get $\exp(-i\Delta) = -1$ and the anti-symmetric orbital u_a changes sign: a phase shift of π between the triplet and singlet orbitals means the same thing than an actual exchange of electron. If we have close collisions which last for a time relatively long, we can define an exchange frequency:

$$\left(\frac{E_s - E_a}{\hbar}\right) = \nu_e \tag{5.46}$$

This obviously means that the phase shift is of several radians during the time of the collision. Furthermore, it is simple to show that, with $\Delta = \pi$, we can write equation (5.34) as:

$$\Psi' = -\frac{1}{\sqrt{2}}[\Psi_K' - \mathscr{E}\Psi_k'] \tag{5.47}$$

where

$$\Psi_k' = u_a(1)\, u_b(2)\, \mathscr{E} F_k \tag{5.48}$$

Effect of spin exchange on the density matrix

The effect of spin exchange on the density matrix elements can be calculated in general for any values of nuclear spins. We would like, however, to limit ourselves to a simple case; we shall thus limit the calculations in this section to the case of hydrogen. The calculations are most illustrative and can be transformed to more complicated cases such as the alkali atoms.

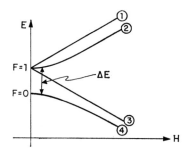

Figure 5.4 Energy levels of H ground state

The hydrogen atom in its ground state $^2S_{1/2}$ possesses a manifold of states as given on figure 5.4.

The difference ΔE is the well known hyperfine energy separation corresponding to a frequency of 1.42 GHz. Let us assume that we have a given distribution of populations between the states and that coherent radiation is applied between states $F = 1$, $M_F = 0$ and $F = 0$, $M_F = 0$. We have numbered the states from highest to lowest. We assume that radiation affects only levels 2 and 4 and we write the initial density matrix as:

$$\varrho_F = \begin{pmatrix} \varrho_{11} & 0 & 0 & 0 \\ 0 & \varrho_{22} & 0 & \varrho_{24} \\ 0 & 0 & \varrho_{33} & 0 \\ 0 & \varrho_{42} & 0 & \varrho_{44} \end{pmatrix} \tag{5.49}$$

The basis for the representation of ϱ is the $F\,M_F$ representation in which the nuclear and electron spins are coupled together to give total angular momentum F. When an interaction occurs between two atoms say 1 and 2, such as in the case of a collision, one picks a representation which is dictated by the problem at hand. In the present case, we want to study electron spin exchange interactions and the best representation, of course, is the one in which the wave functions reflect a coupling between the electron spins which is called the S representation. The total density matrix of the combination $H - H$ in the F representation is:

$$\sigma_F^i = \varrho_F^i \times \varrho_F^i \tag{5.50}$$

which is a 16×16 matrix. The superscript i means initial. Calling Γ the transformation matrix from the F representation to the S representation, we can write:

$$\sigma_s^i = \Gamma \sigma_F^i \Gamma^{-1} \tag{5.51}$$

The matrix $\Gamma = \langle \delta_i \mid F_j \rangle$ is given in table 2. The matrix σ_s can be devided in to 4×4 blocks, with three of them connected with the triplet states and one with the singlet states. This is directly related to figure 5.3. Spin exchange as we have seen earlier corresponds to a phase shift Δ between the triplet and singlet state in the S representation. Call A the following exchange operator:

$$A = \begin{pmatrix} 1 & 0 & 0 & 0 \\ 0 & 1 & 0 & 0 \\ 0 & 0 & 1 & 0 \\ 0 & 0 & 0 & e^{i\Delta} \end{pmatrix} \tag{5.52}$$

where the blocks are 4 × 4 diagonal matrices. The density matrix of the molecule after spin exchange can thus be written:

$$\sigma_s^f = A\sigma_s^i A^{-1} \tag{5.53}$$

where f means final after spin exchange. In order to be able to compare to our initial density matrix ϱ_F^i we have to go back to the initial F representation:

$$\sigma_F^f = \Gamma^{-1} A \Gamma \sigma_F^i \Gamma^{-1} A^{-1} \Gamma \tag{5.54}$$

The task is thus one of calculating $\Gamma^{-1} A \Gamma$ which is the value of A in the F representation. A simple transformation can be made of that last equation in order to obtain a more tractable expression. We define:

$$A = 1 - \frac{X}{4} B \tag{5.55}$$

where

$$X = (1 - \exp(i\varDelta)) \tag{5.56}$$

and B is a 16 × 16 matrix whose elements are all zero except the 4 last ones on the diagonal, which are equal to 4. This permits us to write:

$$\sigma_F^f = \sigma^i - \tfrac{1}{4}(1 - \cos\varDelta)(c\sigma^i + \sigma^i c - \tfrac{1}{2}c\sigma^i c)$$

$$- i\sin\varDelta(\sigma^i c - c\sigma^i) \tag{5.57}$$

where

$$c = \Gamma^{-1} B \Gamma \text{ (see table 3)} \tag{5.58}$$

That is the final result we were looking for. To compare to the initial matrix, one makes a contraction of σ_F^f taking the trace of each 4 × 4 blocks.

One should note that these results, although obtained here to the case of hydrogen, are perfectly general and can be applied to the case of all alkalies. The order of the matrices changes and, of course, in some cases the matrices may become too large to handle. Hydrogen-electron collisions are the simplest case of interest. Hydrogen-hydrogen collisions interest us particularly in relation to the hydrogen maser which we will study later in this chapter.

The final result of the calculations for the case of hydrogen is:

6*

Table 2 $\Gamma = \langle S_i | F_j \rangle$ *Representation Transformation Matrix*

S_eM_e	S_pM_p \ $F_1M_{F_1}\ F_2M_{F_2}$	11 11	11 10	11 1–1	11 00	10 11	10 10	10 1–1	10 00	1–1 11	1–1 10	1–1 1–1	1–1 00	00 11	00 10	00 1–1	00 00
11	11	1	0	0	0	0	0	0	0	0	0	0	0	0	0	0	0
11	10	0	$\frac{1}{2}$	0	$\frac{1}{2}$	$\frac{1}{2}$	0	0	0	0	0	0	0	$\frac{1}{2}$	0	0	0
11	1–1	0	0	0	0	0	$\frac{1}{2}$	0	$\frac{1}{2}$	0	0	0	0	0	$\frac{1}{2}$	0	$\frac{1}{2}$
11	00	0	$\frac{1}{2}$	0	$\frac{1}{2}$	$-\frac{1}{2}$	0	0	0	0	0	0	0	$-\frac{1}{2}$	0	0	0
10	11	0	$\frac{1}{2}$	0	$-\frac{1}{2}$	$\frac{1}{2}$	0	0	0	0	0	0	0	$-\frac{1}{2}$	0	0	0
10	10	0	0	$\frac{1}{2}$	0	0	$\frac{1}{2}$	0	0	$\frac{1}{2}$	0	0	0	0	0	0	$-\frac{1}{2}$
10	1–1	0	0	0	0	0	0	$\frac{1}{2}$	0	0	$\frac{1}{2}$	0	$\frac{1}{2}$	0	0	$\frac{1}{2}$	0
10	00	0	0	$\frac{1}{2}$	0	0	0	0	$\frac{1}{2}$	$-\frac{1}{2}$	0	0	0	0	$-\frac{1}{2}$	0	0
1–1	11	0	0	0	0	0	$\frac{1}{2}$	0	$-\frac{1}{2}$	0	0	0	0	0	$-\frac{1}{2}$	0	$\frac{1}{2}$
1–1	10	0	0	0	0	0	0	$\frac{1}{2}$	0	0	$\frac{1}{2}$	0	$-\frac{1}{2}$	0	0	$-\frac{1}{2}$	0
1–1	1–1	0	0	0	0	0	0	0	0	0	0	1	0	0	0	0	0
1–1	00	0	0	0	0	0	0	$\frac{1}{2}$	0	0	$-\frac{1}{2}$	0	$\frac{1}{2}$	0	0	$-\frac{1}{2}$	0
00	11	0	$\frac{1}{2}$	0	$-\frac{1}{2}$	$-\frac{1}{2}$	0	0	0	0	0	0	0	$\frac{1}{2}$	0	0	0
00	10	0	0	$\frac{1}{2}$	0	0	0	0	$-\frac{1}{2}$	$-\frac{1}{2}$	0	0	0	0	$\frac{1}{2}$	0	0
00	1–1	0	0	0	0	0	0	$\frac{1}{2}$	0	0	$-\frac{1}{2}$	0	$-\frac{1}{2}$	0	0	$\frac{1}{2}$	0
00	00	0	0	$\frac{1}{2}$	0	0	$-\frac{1}{2}$	0	0	$\frac{1}{2}$	0	0	0	0	0	0	$\frac{1}{2}$

Table 3　$C = \Gamma^{*}B\Gamma$

$F_1M_{F_1}$	$F_2M_{F_2}$																	
00	00	0	0	1+	0	0	1−	0	0	1	0	0	0	0	0	0	1
I-I	00	0	0	0	0	0	0	1+	0	0	1−	0	1−	0	0	1	0
0I	00	0	0	1+	0	0	0	0	1−	1−	0	0	0	0	1	0	0
II	00	0	1+	0	1−	1−	0	0	0	0	0	0	0	1	0	0	0
00	I-I	0	0	0	0	0	0	1−	0	0	1	0	1+	0	0	1−	0
I-I	I-I	0	0	0	0	0	0	0	0	0	0	0	0	0	0	0	0
0I	I-I	0	0	0	0	0	0	1−	0	0	1	0	1+	0	0	1−	0
II	I-I	0	0	0	0	0	1−	0	1+	2+	0	0	0	0	1−	0	1−
00	0I	0	0	1−	0	0	0	0	1+	1+	0	0	0	0	1−	0	0
I-I	0I	0	0	0	0	0	0	1+	0	0	1−	0	1−	0	0	1	0
0I	0I	0	0	1−	0	0	1+	0	0	1−	0	0	0	0	0	0	1−
II	0I	0	1−	0	1+	1+	0	0	0	0	0	0	0	1−	0	0	0
00	II	0	1−	0	1+	1+	0	0	0	0	0	0	0	1−	0	0	0
I-I	II	0	0	2	0	0	1−	0	1−	0	0	0	0	0	1	0	1
0I	II	0	1+	0	1−	1−	0	0	0	0	0	0	0	1	0	0	0
II	II	0	0	0	0	0	0	0	0	0	0	0	0	0	0	0	0
$F_2M_{F_2}$		11	10	1-1	00	11	10	1-1	00	11	10	1-1	00	11	10	1-1	00
$F_1M_{F_1}$		11	11	11	11	10	10	10	10	1-1	1-1	1-1	1-1	00	00	00	00

$$\tilde{\varrho}_{11} = \varrho_{11} - \frac{(1 - \cos\varDelta)}{2} \left\{ \varrho_{11} - \frac{(1 + P)^2}{4} + \frac{|\varrho_{42}|^2}{2} \right\} \tag{5.59}$$

$$\tilde{\varrho}_{22} = \varrho_{22} - \frac{(1 - \cos\varDelta)}{2} \left\{ \varrho_{22} - \frac{(1 - P^2)}{4} - \frac{|\varrho_{42}|^2}{2} \right\} \tag{5.60}$$

$$\tilde{\varrho}_{33} = \varrho_{33} - \frac{(1 - \cos\varDelta)}{2} \left\{ \varrho_{33} - \frac{(1 - P)^2}{4} + \frac{|\varrho_{42}|^2}{2} \right\} \tag{5.61}$$

$$\tilde{\varrho}_{44} = \varrho_{44} - \frac{(1 - \cos\varDelta)}{2} \left\{ \varrho_{44} - \frac{(1 - P)^2}{4} - \frac{|\varrho_{42}|^2}{2} \right\} \tag{5.62}$$

$$\tilde{\varrho}_{42} = \varrho_{42} - \frac{(1 - \cos\varDelta)}{4} \varrho_{42} - \frac{i}{4} \sin\varDelta \varrho_{42}(\varrho_{22} - \varrho_{44}) \tag{5.63}$$

$$\tilde{\varrho}_{24} = \varrho_{24} - \frac{(1 - \cos\varDelta)}{4} \varrho_{24} + \frac{i}{4} \sin\varDelta \varrho_{24}(\varrho_{22} - \varrho_{44}) \tag{5.64}$$

The tilda on the ϱ's means an average over collision times with consequence that terms which contain factors oscillating at frequency high relative to the inverse of the averaging time are zero. The symbol P stands for the polarization $(\varrho_{11} - \varrho_{33})$.

In most cases we are interested in rates of change of the various elements $\varrho_{\alpha\alpha'}$. For example, a very important case is the rate of change of $(\varrho_{22} - \varrho_{44})$ which can be written:

$$\left(\frac{d(\varrho_{22} - \varrho_{44})}{dt} \right)_{se} = - \left(\begin{matrix} \text{number of collisions} \\ \text{per second} \end{matrix} \right) \left(\begin{matrix} \text{change in } (\varrho_{22} - \varrho_{44}) \\ \text{per collision} \end{matrix} \right)$$

$$= -S[(\varrho_{22} - \varrho_{44})^i - (\varrho_{22} - \varrho_{44})^f] \tag{5.65}$$

where S is the number of collisions per second.

In the case $\varDelta = \pi$, complete spin exchange, we may write that parameter simply as:

$$S = n\bar{v}_r \sigma \tag{5.66}$$

where n is the density, $\bar{v}_r$ the relative velocity and σ the spin exchange cross section.

In that case we obtain:

$$\left(\frac{d(\varrho_{22} - \varrho_{44})}{dt} \right)_{s.e.} = -n\bar{v}_r \sigma (\varrho_{22} - \varrho_{44}) \tag{5.67}$$

For the off-diagonal elements we get:

$$\left(\frac{d\varrho_{42}}{dt}\right)_{s.e.} = -\frac{n\bar{v}_r\sigma}{2}\varrho_{42} \tag{5.68}$$

It should be noted that the polarization P does not change upon spin exchange collisions as can be verified by direct substraction of equation (5.61) from equation (5.59). In the case in which we let Δ take any value, we have to average over those values of Δ to define a new σ.

$$\sigma_{ex} = \tfrac{1}{2}[\sigma(1 - \cos\Delta)]_{av}. \tag{5.69}$$

Equation (5.67) still holds but we have to include in equation (5.68) the complex term which introduces a frequency shift in the transition ω_{24}.

5.3 MOLECULAR AMPLIFIERS

In section 4.7 we have developed a theory of stimulated emission; energy could be drawn out of an ensemble of spins and, in fact, we obtained the basic principles underlying the operation of a molecular amplifier. We have shown that in some specific circumstances we could obtain an actual oscillation which was growing up to a certain value after excitation. That was an oscillation that could be sustained if a replenishment of the population inversion could be performed.

We would like to apply the principles developed in that section to calculate the steady state operation of two typical atomic oscillators, a beam maser and an optically pumped maser.

A BEAM MASER As an example of a beam maser, we will calculate the condition for steady state operation of the hydrogen maser.

The hydrogen maser works in the following way. A beam of atomic hydrogen is formed from a molecular hydrogen dissociator. That beam is made to pass in a magnetic field gradient of a given symmetry (hexapole magnet) which, referring to figure 5.4 of section 5.2, focuses on the beam axis, atoms in state (1) and (2), or $F = 1$, $M_F = 1, 0$. These atoms enter in a storage bulb which is itself placed inside a microwave cavity tuned to the hyperfine frequency of hydrogen (1420 MHz). The storage bulb serves to maintain the atoms in a field of constant phase reducing first order doppler effect to a negligible amount; it is coated internally with a substance which prevents relaxation upon collision of an atom on the inside surface (teflon or wax). Relaxation times of the order of one second can be achieved

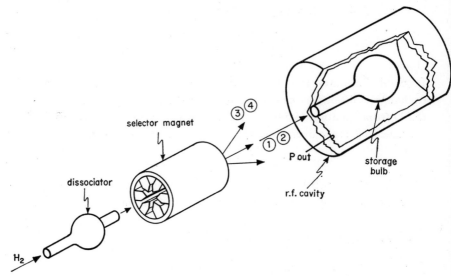

Figure 5.5 Schematic diagram of a hydrogen maser

that way, with corresponding line widths of one cycle per second. A drawing of the maser is shown on figure 5.5.

The equilibrium density matrix in the bulb is taken as equation (5.49) from section 5.2.

It is:

$$\varrho = \begin{pmatrix} \varrho_{11} & 0 & 0 & 0 \\ 0 & \varrho_{22} & 0 & \varrho_{24} \\ 0 & 0 & \varrho_{33} & 0 \\ 0 & \varrho_{42} & 0 & \varrho_{44} \end{pmatrix} \tag{5.70}$$

The rate of change of any element in the bulb is given by:

$$\frac{d\varrho}{dt} = \left(\frac{d\varrho}{dt}\right)_{flow} + \left(\frac{d\varrho}{dt}\right)_{wall} + \left(\frac{d\varrho}{dt}\right)_{s.e.} + \left(\frac{d\varrho}{dt}\right)_{rad} \tag{5.71}$$

Other terms could be added phenomenologically in the same way. However we shall limit ourselves to those terms. Each term is now written explicitly:

Flow

$$\left(\frac{d\varrho}{dt}\right)_{flow} = \begin{pmatrix} \dfrac{I_1}{N} & 0 & 0 & 0 \\ 0 & \dfrac{I_2}{N} & 0 & 0 \\ 0 & 0 & 0 & 0 \\ 0 & 0 & 0 & 0 \end{pmatrix} - \gamma_b \varrho \tag{5.72}$$

The first elements represent the beam flux in the two proper levels entering the bulb, normalized to the total number of atoms in the bulb; the second term describes the atoms coming out. At equilibrium, if $I_t = I_1 + I_2$ is the total beam flux, we can write:

$$\frac{I_t}{N} = \gamma_b \left(\varrho_{11}^0 + \varrho_{22}^0 \right) = \gamma_b \tag{5.73}$$

or

$$\frac{I_1}{N} = \frac{I_2}{N} = \frac{1}{2} \gamma_b \quad \text{(for } I_1 = I_2\text{)} \tag{5.74}$$

The zero on ϱ means that no other perturbations are considered in that definition.

Spin Exchange   The equations describing spin exchange interactions have been obtained earlier. We shall be interested primarily in the rate of change of $(\varrho_{22} - \varrho_{44})$ and ϱ_{24}. We have for those:

$$\frac{d(\varrho_{22} - \varrho_{44})}{dt} = -\gamma_e u (\varrho_{22} - \varrho_{44}) \tag{5.75}$$

$$\frac{d\varrho_{42}}{dt} = -\frac{u}{2} \gamma_e \varrho_{42} - \frac{i\gamma_e}{2} v \varrho_{42} (\varrho_{22} - \varrho_{44}) \tag{5.76}$$

where

$$u = \frac{\overline{(1 - \cos \Delta)}}{2} \tag{5.77}$$

$$v = \frac{\overline{\sin \Delta}}{2} \tag{5.78}$$

$$\gamma_e = n \bar{v}_r \sigma \tag{5.79}$$

Radiation   With the degeneracy lifted by a small d.c. field, we write for the proper transition:

$$\mathcal{H}_{42} = \hbar \beta \exp(i\omega t) \tag{5.80}$$

where

$$\beta = \frac{\mu_0 H_z}{2\hbar} \tag{5.81}$$

in which H_z is the applied r.f. field and μ_0 is the value of Bohr's magneton. In all that follows we shall assume that the atoms see the average field $\langle H_z \rangle$; this is justified since in that type of maser the atoms move randomly in the storage bulb and traverses this bulb several times during the time of interaction with H_1. Using equation (2.58) of chapter 2, we obtain

$$\frac{d(\varrho_{22} - \varrho_{44})}{dt} = 4\langle \beta \rangle \operatorname{Im} \varrho_{42} \exp(-i\omega t) \tag{5.82}$$

$$\frac{d\varrho_{42}}{dt} = i\omega_0\varrho_{42} - i\langle \beta \rangle (\varrho_{22} - \varrho_{44}) \exp(i\omega t) \tag{5.83}$$

Wall Relaxation   Wall relaxation is not too well understood except in very special cases. For this reason, we assume uniform relaxation with equal rates for diagonal elements and off-diagonal elements. That assumption does not describe exactly the experimental situation but it is good enough for our purpose. We thus write $d\varrho/dt = \gamma_w\varrho$ for the effect of the walls on the matrix elements.

We have thus all the information needed to state our problem in two equations:

$$\frac{d(\varrho_{22} - \varrho_{44})}{dt} = \frac{1}{2}\gamma_b - \gamma_b (\varrho_{22} - \varrho_{44}) - \gamma_w(\varrho_{22} - \varrho_{44})$$
$$- \gamma_e u(\varrho_{22} - \varrho_{44}) + 4\langle \beta \rangle \operatorname{Im} \varrho_{42} \exp(-i\omega t) \tag{5.84}$$

$$\frac{d(\varrho_{42})}{dt} = -\gamma_b \varrho_{42} - \gamma_w\varrho_{42} - \frac{\gamma_e}{2} u\varrho_{42} - \frac{i\gamma_e}{2} v\varrho_{42}(\varrho_{22} - \varrho_{44})$$
$$+ i\omega_0\varrho_{42} - i\langle \beta \rangle (\varrho_{22} - \varrho_{44}) \exp(i\omega t) \tag{5.85}$$

Those two equations have to be solved simultaneously. We assume equilibrium, that is, a steady state in which $d(\varrho_{22} - \varrho_{44})/dt = 0$, or we assume that the population difference between levels (2) and (4) does not vary with time. We also assume that ϱ_{42} has a solution of the form:

$$\varrho_{42} = \delta \exp(i\omega t) \tag{5.86}$$

From these two assumptions, it is then simple mathematics to show that

$$(\varrho_{22} - \varrho_{44}) = \frac{\frac{1}{2}\gamma_b}{\gamma_1 + \dfrac{4\langle \beta \rangle^2 \gamma_2}{\gamma_1^2 + (\omega' - \omega)^2}} \tag{5.87}$$

and

$$\operatorname{Im} \delta = -\frac{\frac{1}{2}\langle \beta \rangle \gamma_b}{\gamma_1\gamma_2 + \dfrac{\gamma_1}{\gamma_2}(\omega' - \omega)^2 + 4\langle \beta \rangle^2} \tag{5.88}$$

where

$$\omega' = \omega_0 - \frac{\gamma_e v}{2}(\varrho_{22} - \varrho_{44}) \tag{5.89}$$

$$\gamma_1 = \gamma_b + \gamma_w + \gamma_e u \tag{5.90}$$

$$\gamma_2 = \gamma_b + \gamma_w + \frac{\gamma_e}{2} u \tag{5.91}$$

The power delivered by the atoms is given by:

$$P_{at} = \hbar \omega N \left(\frac{d\varrho_{22}}{dt}\right)_{rad} \tag{5.92}$$

where N is the total number of atoms in the bulb. With the value obtained above for Im δ we finally obtain:

$$P_{at} = \frac{1}{2}\hbar \omega I_{tot} \frac{2\langle\beta\rangle^2}{\gamma_1\gamma_2 + \frac{\gamma_1}{\gamma_2}(\omega' - \omega)^2 + 4\langle\beta\rangle^2} \tag{5.93}$$

In order to verify if sustained oscillations are possible, we use the technique developed earlier. We equate the power delivered by the atoms to the power dissipated in the cavity which we have written as:

$$P_{dis} = \frac{\omega V_c}{8\pi Q} \frac{\hbar^2}{\mu_0^2 \eta} 4\langle\beta\rangle^2 \tag{5.94}$$

Using the following definitions:

$$I_{th} = \frac{\hbar V_c(\gamma_b + \gamma_w)^2}{4\pi\mu_0^2 Q \eta} \tag{5.95}$$

$$P_c = \frac{\omega\hbar^2 V_c(\gamma_b + \gamma_w)^2}{8\pi\mu_0^2 Q \eta} \tag{5.96}$$

we finally obtain:

$$P = P_c \left\{\frac{I}{I_{th}} - \frac{\gamma_1\gamma_2}{(\gamma_b + \gamma_w)^2}\right\} \tag{5.97}$$

where I is the actual atomic flux in state 2. One notes that γ_1 and γ_2 depend on the beam flux through spin exchange interaction which is density dependent. We can rewrite γ_e as:

$$\gamma_e = \frac{I\bar{v}_r\sigma}{(\gamma_b + \varepsilon\gamma_w) V_b} \frac{I_{total}}{I} \tag{5.98}$$

where $\varepsilon\gamma_\omega$ is the part of wall relaxation which is recombination and which appears effectively as a hole for the atom. We define a quality factor parameter:

$$q = \frac{\sigma V_r \hbar}{8\pi\mu_0^2} \frac{\gamma_b + \gamma_w}{\gamma_b + \varepsilon\gamma_w} \frac{V_c}{\eta V_b} \frac{1}{Q} \frac{I_{tot}}{I} \qquad (5.99)$$

which effectively is a measure of the strength of the spin exchange interaction, through σ, the cross section. The final result obtained is:

$$\boxed{\frac{P}{P_c} = \left\{ -2q^2 \left(\frac{I}{I_{th}}\right)^2 + (1 - 3q)\frac{I}{I_{th}} - 1\right\}} \qquad (5.100)$$

That equation describes the steady state operation of the hydrogen maser oscillating between the state $F = 1$, $M_F = 0$ and $F = 0$, $M_F = 0$. It is observed that oscillations are possible only for beam fluxes between the extreme values:

$$I_\pm = I_{th} \left\{ \frac{(1 - 4q) \pm [(1 - 4q)^2 - 16q^2]^{1/2}}{8q^2} \right\} \qquad (5.101)$$

That equation will have real positive values only for $q < 0.172$ which puts constraints mainly on the Q of the cavity and on the filling factor.

B OPTICALLY PUMPED MASERS The optically pumped maser differs essentially from the beam maser through the fact that the population inversion in the ground state is obtained through optical pumping rather than by magnetic or electrostatic selection on a beam. As an example of such a maser, we will take the case of the rubidium maser which has proved to be successful.

A schematic diagram of the rubidium maser is shown in figure 5.6. It consists essentially of a quartz cell containing nitrogen at a pressure of 11 Torr and the isotope Rb^{87}. The cell is enclosed in a high Q cavity. Light from an Rb^{87} lamp, filtered by a cell containing Rb^{85}, penetrates inside the cavity and orients the Rb^{87} atoms. The energy levels of the rubidium atom are shown in figure 5.7. The purpose of the Rb^{85} filter is to remove from the spectrum of the Rb^{87} lamp the line at the frequency corresponding to the transitions from the P state to the level $F = 2$ of the ground state. After the rubidium atoms have been excited to the P state, they are relaxed to both levels $F = 1$ and $F = 2$ of the ground state by collisions with nitrogen molecules. Because of the asymmetry in the pumping light, a net population unbalance is obtained. When enough atoms are "pumped" into the upper level $F = 2$, self-sustained oscillations are observed between the $F = 2$, $M_F = 0$ and $F = 1$, $M_F = 0$ levels at a frequency of 6.835 GHz.

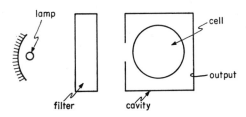

Figure 5.6   Schematic diagram of a Rb maser

In order to obtain a mathematical closed-form solution of the operation of the maser, the following assumptions are made:

1.   Reradiation is completely quenched by the nitrogen buffer gas.

2.   The decay from the excited states takes place randomly with equal probability to any of the ground states.

3.   In the ground state, in the absence of light, relaxation taking place through collisions produces an equilibrium situation with all atoms equally distributed among the eight Zeeman sublevels shown in figure 5.7.

4.   The incident light consists of one simple hyperfine line $P - S(F = 1)$; in other words we assume an ideal Rb^{85} filter.

The theory describes the operation of an ideal maser which would operate according to those assumptions.

Master Equations   The equilibrium density matrix ϱ in the laboratory frame of reference is written for the ground state as:

$$\varrho = \begin{pmatrix} \varrho_{11} & 0 & 0 & 0 & 0 & 0 & 0 & 0 \\ 0 & \varrho_{22} & 0 & 0 & 0 & 0 & 0 & 0 \\ 0 & 0 & \varrho_{33} & 0 & 0 & 0 & \varrho_{37} & 0 \\ 0 & 0 & 0 & \varrho_{44} & 0 & 0 & 0 & 0 \\ 0 & 0 & 0 & 0 & \varrho_{55} & 0 & 0 & 0 \\ 0 & 0 & 0 & 0 & 0 & \varrho_{66} & 0 & 0 \\ 0 & 0 & \varrho_{73} & 0 & 0 & 0 & \varrho_{77} & 0 \\ 0 & 0 & 0 & 0 & 0 & 0 & 0 & \varrho_{88} \end{pmatrix} \qquad (5.102)$$

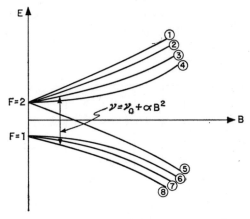

Figure 5.7 Ground state energy levels of a rubidium 87 atom. In the maser, B is a few milligauss and the levels are well separated.

The hyperfine levels are numbered from high to low energy. It is assumed that the transition takes place between the field-independent levels (3) and (7). The rate of change of any element is given by

$$\frac{d\varrho}{dt} = \left(\frac{d\varrho}{dt}\right)_{op} + \left(\frac{d\varrho}{dt}\right)_{rel} + \left(\frac{d\varrho}{dt}\right)_{rad} \tag{5.103}$$

where $(d\varrho/dt)_{op}$ is the change with time of any element due to the pumping light; $(d\varrho/dt)_{rel}$ is the change with time of any element due to relaxation processes in the ground states; the processes include, for example, collisions between rubidium atoms and nitrogen molecules and rubidium-rubidium spin-exchange collisions; $(d\varrho/dt)_{rad}$ is the change with time caused by r.f. radiation.

1 OPTICAL PUMPING   The effect of the light on the density matrix elements is given by the following expressions derived earlier in this chapter:

$$\frac{d\varrho'_{\mu\mu'}}{dt} = -\left\{\left(\frac{\Gamma_\mu}{2} + i\delta^l_\mu\right) + \left(\frac{\Gamma_{\mu'}}{2} - i\delta^l_{\mu'}\right)\right\}\varrho'_{\mu\mu'} \tag{5.104}$$

where Γ_α is the term proportional to the light intensity and the cross section for absorption of a photon by an atom; $\delta^l_{\alpha'}$ are frequency shifts produced by the radiation field. In the present case, due to assumption 4, we have:

$$\Gamma_\mu = 0 \quad \text{for} \quad \mu = 1, 2, 3, 4, 5 \tag{5.105}$$

We define:

$$\Gamma_\mu = \Gamma(z, r) \quad \text{for} \quad \mu = 6, 7, 8 \tag{5.106}$$

$$\delta_3^l - \delta_7^l = \Delta\omega_l(z, r) = \text{light shift} \tag{5.107}$$

In the analysis, z is the direction of the magnetic field and of incidence of the light; r is a distance in the cavity measured from the axis of symmetry. The pumping rate Γ, the density matrix element ϱ, and the light shift $\Delta\omega_l$ are all functions of the distance of penetration of the light inside the maser cell. Actually, Γ can be written

$$\Gamma(z, r) = \int_0^\infty I(\nu, z, r)\, \sigma(\nu)\, d\nu \tag{5.108}$$

where $I(\nu, z, r)$ is the light intensity at frequency ν, and position (z, r) in the maser cell, and $\sigma(\nu)$ is the cross section for absorption of a photon. The rate equations can be written with ϱ, $\Gamma \Delta\omega_l$ functions of z and r as:

$$\left(\frac{d\varrho_{\mu\mu}}{dt}\right)_{op} = -\Gamma\varrho_{\mu\mu}, \quad \mu = 6, 7, 8 \tag{5.109}$$

$$\left(\frac{d\varrho_{73}}{dt}\right)_{op} = -\frac{1}{2}\Gamma\varrho_{73} - i\Delta\omega_l\varrho_{73} \tag{5.110}$$

In this context, for a given light intensity I_0 incident on the cell, Γ expressed in photons per atom per second is a function of temperature, because a certain amount of light is lost to counteract relaxation in the maser. However, the medium becomes transparent, to some extent, upon optical pumping, and the light penetrates into the central region of the cavity. In other words, the mean free path of the light inside the cell is increased by the light itself due to its unsymmetrical nature. Γ is thus a parameter which is fixed for a given situation; it is best determined by a measurement on the maser itself.

2 RELAXATION The master equation for relaxation has been obtained aerlier:

$$\frac{d\varrho_{\mu\mu}}{dt} = \frac{1}{\hbar^2} \sum_{\mu'} [J_{\mu'\mu}(\omega_{\mu'\mu})\, \varrho_{\mu'\mu'} - J_{\mu\mu'}(\omega_{\mu\mu'})\, \varrho_{\mu\mu}] \tag{5.111}$$

we define $\gamma_1 = 8J_{\beta\alpha}/\hbar^2$ and assume uniform relaxation among all the eight levels. That permits us to write:

$$\frac{d\varrho_{\mu\mu}}{dt} = -\gamma_1\left(\varrho_{\mu\mu} - \frac{1}{8}\right) \tag{5.112}$$

The decay of the off-diagonal elements is characterized by a rate γ_2:

$$\frac{d\varrho_{\mu\mu'}}{dt} = -\gamma_2 \varrho_{\mu\mu'} \tag{5.113}$$

Both γ_1 and γ_2 contain contributions from buffer-gas collisions, spin-exchange collisions and collisions between rubidium atoms and the wall of the storage cell. Any other relaxation mechanism can be introduced in a similar phenomenological way. γ_1 and γ_2 are respectively $1/T_1$ and $1/T_2$.

3   RADIATION   The radiation term is calculated as in the case of the beam maser. However, due to the assumption that the atoms are fixed in space, fields cannot be averaged in the same way. Each atom sees a field of a given magnitude at position (zr).

From these mechanisms a set of eight equations is written for the diagonal elements of the density matrix. One equation is sufficient for the off-diagonal element, ϱ_{73}. Those equations are:

$$\frac{d\varrho_{\mu\mu}}{dt} = \frac{1}{8}\Gamma(\varrho_{66} + \varrho_{77} + \varrho_{88}) - \gamma_1\left(\varrho_{\mu\mu} - \frac{1}{8}\right) \tag{5.114}$$

for $\mu = 1, 2, 4, 5$;

$$\frac{d\varrho_{33}}{dt} = \frac{1}{8}\Gamma(\varrho_{66} + \varrho_{77} + \varrho_{88}) - \gamma_1\left(\varrho_{33} - \frac{1}{8}\right) + 2\beta\operatorname{Im}\varrho_{73}\exp\left(-i\omega t\right) \tag{5.115}$$

$$\frac{d\varrho_{\mu\mu}}{dt} = \Gamma\varrho_{\mu\mu} + \frac{1}{8}\Gamma(\varrho_{66} + \varrho_{77} + \varrho_{88}) - \gamma_1\left(\varrho_{\mu\mu} - \frac{1}{8}\right) \tag{5.116}$$

for $\mu = 6, 8$;

$$\frac{d\varrho_{77}}{dt} = \Gamma\varrho_{77} + \frac{1}{8}\Gamma(\varrho_{66} + \varrho_{77} + \varrho_{88}) - \gamma_1\left(\varrho_{77} - \frac{1}{8}\right)$$
$$- 2\beta\operatorname{Im}\varrho_{73}\exp\left(-i\omega t\right) \tag{5.117}$$

$$\frac{d\varrho_{73}}{dt} = i\omega_0\varrho_{73} - i\beta(\varrho_{33} - \varrho_{77})\exp\left(i\omega t\right) - \left(\frac{1}{2}\Gamma + \gamma_2\right)\varrho_{37} - i\Delta\,\omega_1\varrho_{73} \tag{5.118}$$

where ω is the frequency of the applied field H_z, ω_0 is the atomic resonant frequency and $\beta = \frac{1}{2}(\mu_0 H_z/\hbar)$ a function of (zr).

The solution of this set of equations is done at equilibrium as in the case of the hydrogen maser. The power delivered by the rubidium vapor contained in the element dv at position (zr) is given by $n\,dvh\nu(d\varrho_{33}/dt)_{rad}$ and is calculated as

$$dP = nh\nu\,dv$$

$$\times \frac{2\beta^2\Gamma A}{\gamma_1(\tfrac{1}{2}\Gamma + \gamma_2) + [\gamma_1/(\tfrac{1}{2}\Gamma + \gamma_2)](\omega - \omega')^2 + (1 - \Gamma B)\,4\beta^2} \qquad (5.119)$$

where

$$A = \gamma_1(\Gamma + \gamma_1)/(5\Gamma^2 + 13\gamma_1\Gamma + 8\gamma_1^2) \qquad (5.120)$$

$$B = (3\Gamma + 4\gamma_1)/(5\Gamma^2 + 13\gamma_1\Gamma + 8\gamma_1^2) \qquad (5.121)$$

$$\omega' = \omega_0 - \Delta\omega_l \qquad (5.122)$$

The field created by the rubidium atoms has to be made self consistant. This is done again by equating the radiated power to the dissipated power. However due to the form of equation (5.119), the total power emitted by the atoms cannot be obtained in an analytical form by simple calculus. That equation with parameters depending on (zr) can be integrated only by numerical methods. To obtain a close form analytical solution of the maser equation, we shall make the following approximation. We shall average the terms Γ, ω', and β^2 individually and write $\int n\,dv$ as N the total number of atoms. The expression obtained is then exact for the case where Γ, ω' and β are uniform over the volume occupied by the ensemble. Although those are crude assumptions, the final result obtained should, however, give the general behaviour of the device and exhibit the important parameters. The final result is the maser equation:

$$\frac{P}{P_m} = \left[\frac{\Gamma'}{\Gamma'_m}\,\frac{\Gamma' + 1}{(2\Gamma'^2 + 9\Gamma' + 8)} - \frac{(\tfrac{1}{2}\Gamma' + r)(5\Gamma'^2 + 13\Gamma' + 8)}{(2\Gamma'^2 + 9\Gamma' + 8)}\right] \qquad (5.123)$$

where

$$\Gamma'_m = \frac{\gamma_1\hbar}{4n\pi Q_l\eta\mu_0^2} \qquad (5.124)$$

$$\Gamma' = \frac{\Gamma}{\gamma_1} \qquad (5.125)$$

$$P_m = \tfrac{1}{2}Nh\nu\Gamma_m \qquad (5.126)$$

$$r = \frac{\gamma_2}{\gamma_1} \qquad (5.127)$$

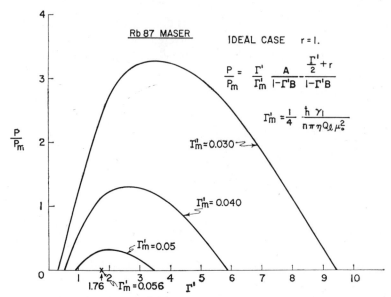

Figure 5.8 Variation of power output of the rubidium maser versus light intensity for several values of the oscillation parameter Γ'_m.

The various parameters are defined as follows: n is the rubidium density; N is the total number of atoms; Q_l is the cavity quality factor; η is the filling factor now defined as $\langle H_z^2 \rangle / \langle H_{rf}^2 \rangle$; μ_0 is the Bohr magneton; ν is the resonance frequency. Figure 5.8 shows the variation of P/P_m with the normalized pumping rate Γ' for several values of Γ'_m.

Γ'_m is called the oscillation parameter in a sense similar to q in the hydrogen maser. By requiring the power output to be positive (oscillating state) we can set a limit on Γ'_m. That limit is:

$$\Gamma'_m \leq [(\sqrt{80r}) + 4 + 5r]^{-1} \tag{5.128}$$

In order to determine if oscillations are possible, one needs to know the ratio of γ_2 to γ_1. Experiments have shown that in a buffer gas such as nitrogen, dephasing collisions are more frequent than collisions which affect the populations of the states. Thus at low rubidium pressures where the spin-exchange dephasing action between rubidium atoms is small relative to interactions with the buffer gas, we expect r to be large. At temperatures of the order of 65° C where spin-exchange interactions contribute to a large extent to the relaxation, one finds experimentally that r is close to 1. Consequently, the minimum value of $\Gamma_{m'}$ necessary for oscillation varies with the density of rubidium. In the case $r = 1$, $\Gamma'_{m'}$ needs to be smaller than 0.056.

5.4 THE LASER

In this last section we give a simple theory of the basic principles governing the operation of the laser.* The theory of operation of that device goes along the general lines of the theories developed earlier for the case of the hydrogen and rubidium masers. There is one essential difference, however, which arises due to the short wavelength involved at the optical frequencies. The resonator used is then different in construction; it consists of two plane mirrors placed at a distance which may vary from centimeters to meters and which form a Fabry-Perot arrangement as shown in figure 5.9.

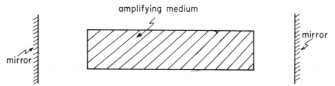

Figure 5.9 Fabry–Perot arrangement for a laser.

An intense oscillating electric field can be created in the region between the mirrors. In the single mode approximation, that field may be described by the expression:

$$E_n(zt) = A_n(t)\, U_n(z) \tag{5.129}$$

where

$$A_n(t) = E_n^0 \cos \omega_n t \tag{5.130}$$

$$U_n(z) = \sin k_n z \tag{5.131}$$

with

$$k_n = \frac{2\pi}{\lambda} = \frac{n\pi}{L} \tag{5.132}$$

The number n is very large, of the order of 2×10^6. In the analysis we shall assume single axial mode operation with the angular frequency:

$$\Omega_n = \frac{n\pi c}{L} \tag{5.133}$$

---

* In this section we shall follow the main lines of the theory developed by W. Lamb jr. (see reference in bibliography). We shall not go in all details however; we shall only develop the oscillating conditions.

6a*

That mode possesses the highest Q.

The amplifying medium is placed between the mirrors and may have an energy level structure as shown in figure 5.10.

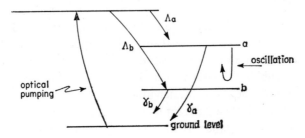

Figure 5.10   Energy level scheme used in the present analysis.

Atoms are pumped from the ground state to high excited states. These atoms may then relax to state (a) and (b), according to standard notation, at rates Λ_a and Λ_b. Levels (a) and (b) are the two levels between which an oscillating electric dipole exists and which gives the coherent radiation. We also associate with these levels phenomenological decay rates γ_a and γ_b to the ground state.

In the gaseous laser the problem is complicated by the fact that atoms are moving randomly and see a doppler shifted frequency. Since we are interested mostly in the essential characteristics of operation of the laser, we will limit ourselves to the simple case where the atoms are assumed to be at rest. This may, for example, apply to the case of a solid. Furthermore, we assume Λ_a and Λ_b constant in time and independent of position, somewhat as we did for the case of the rubidium maser pumping rate Γ. The rate equations for the density matrix elements for atoms at position z are then:

$$\frac{d\varrho_{aa}}{dt} = -\gamma_a\varrho_{aa} + 2\,\mathrm{Im}\,\frac{\mathcal{H}_{ab}}{\hbar}\varrho_{ba} + \Lambda_a \tag{5.134}$$

$$\frac{d\varrho_{bb}}{dt} = -\gamma_b\varrho_{bb} - 2\,\mathrm{Im}\,\frac{\mathcal{H}_{ab}}{\hbar}\varrho_{ba} + \Lambda_b \tag{5.135}$$

$$\frac{d\varrho_{ba}}{dt} = -\gamma_{ab}\varrho_{ba} + i\omega_0\varrho_{ba} - i\frac{\mathcal{H}_{ba}}{\hbar}(\varrho_{aa} - \varrho_{bb}) \tag{5.136}$$

where $\mathcal{H}_{ab}$ is the matrix element of the interaction between the atoms and the electric field. Much as we did for the case of the hydrogen and rubidium masers we solve this set of equations at equilibrium for which the derivative of each element is equal to zero. We assume a solution for which:

$$\varrho_{ba} = \delta\, e^{i\omega t} \tag{5.137}$$

Using the rotating wave approximation in which we neglect rapidly varying exponentials we get:

$$\varDelta = \varrho_{aa} - \varrho_{bb} = \frac{2}{\gamma'}\, \mathrm{Im}\,\delta + \mathscr{N} \tag{5.138}$$

$$\delta = -\frac{(\omega_n - \omega_0)\,\mathscr{E}\varDelta}{\gamma_{ab}^2 + (\omega_n - \omega_0)^2} - i\frac{\gamma_{ab}\mathscr{E}\varDelta}{\gamma_{ab}^2 + (\omega_n - \omega_0)^2} \tag{5.139}$$

where

$$\gamma' = \frac{\gamma_a\gamma_b}{\gamma_a + \gamma_b} \tag{5.140}$$

$$\mathscr{N} = \frac{\varLambda_a}{\gamma_a} - \frac{\varLambda_b}{\gamma_b} \tag{5.141}$$

$$\gamma_{ab} = \tfrac{1}{2}(\gamma_a + \gamma_b) \tag{5.142}$$

and $\mathscr{E}$ represents the interaction containing the electric dipole matrix element μ between levels (a) and (b):

$$\mathscr{E} = \frac{\mu E_n^0}{2\hbar}\, U(z) \tag{5.143}$$

Those equations being combined give:

$$\varDelta = \frac{\mathscr{N}}{1 + \dfrac{2\gamma_{ab}/\gamma'\mathscr{E}^2}{\gamma_{ab}^2 + (\omega_n - \omega_0)^2}} \tag{5.144}$$

$$\delta = -\frac{(\omega_n - \omega_0)\,\mathscr{E}}{\gamma_{ab}^2 + (\omega_n - \omega_0)^2 + 2\gamma_{ab}/\gamma'\mathscr{E}^2}$$

$$- i\frac{\gamma_{ab}\mathscr{E}}{\gamma_{ab}^2 + (\omega_n - \omega_0)^2 + 2\gamma_{ab}/\gamma'\mathscr{E}^2} \tag{5.145}$$

which exhibit, as in the case of magnetic transitions, the effect of saturation at the optical frequencies. The polarization of atoms at position z is obtained as:

$$\mathscr{P}(z, t) = (\varrho_{ab} + \varrho_{ba}) \tag{5.146}$$

7   Vanier (3034)

If we assume resonance between the applied frequency and the atomic frequency, we obtain:

$$\mathscr{P}(z, t) = 2 \frac{\gamma_{ab}\mathscr{E}}{\gamma_{ab}^2 + 2\gamma_{ab}/\gamma'^2\varepsilon^2} \sin \omega_0 t \qquad (5.147)$$

This is one of the basis equations of the analysis.

In order to obtain the oscillation condition we must find a relation between the energy delivered by the atoms and the energy lost in the resonator; in the present case we can obtain a classical relation between the polarization in the atomic system and the electric field in the resonator. We assume a lossy medium with an ohmic conductivity σ giving the desired damping of the normal mode; σ includes the losses through the mirror made semitransparent in order to couple out some of the energy. In that case a proper combination of Maxwell's equations gives us:

$$-\frac{\partial^2 E_n(z, t)}{\partial z^2} + \mu_0\sigma \frac{\partial E_n(z, t)}{\partial t} + \mu_0\varepsilon_0 \frac{\partial^2 E_n(z, t)}{\partial t^2} = -\mu_0 \frac{\partial^2 \mathscr{P}_n(z, t)}{\partial t^2}$$

$$(5.148)$$

where we have assumed E constant in the x and y directions. Using equation (5.129) and (5.130), we obtain:

$$\frac{d^2 A_n}{dt^2} + \frac{\omega_n}{Q_n} \frac{dA_n}{dt} + \Omega_n^2 A_n = -\frac{1}{\varepsilon_0} \frac{d^2 \mathscr{P}_n(t)}{dt^2} \qquad (5.149)$$

where

$$\mathscr{P}_n(t) = \frac{2}{L} \int_0^L \mathscr{P}_n(zt) \sin k_n z \, dz \qquad (5.150)$$

$$Q_n = \frac{\varepsilon_0 \omega_n}{\sigma} \qquad (5.151)$$

We assume a solution of the form:

$$\mathscr{P}_n(t) = S_n \sin \omega_n t \qquad (5.152)$$

which, when replaced in equation (5.149), gives the relation between the field, the polarization and the frequencies:

$$E_n^0 = -\frac{Q_n}{\varepsilon_0} S_n \qquad (5.153)$$

$$\omega_n = \Omega_n \qquad (5.154)$$

That last equation was forced upon us by the form of equation (5.152) which sets the polarization in quadrature with the field. It is thus a restriction which prevents us from obtaining information on frequency pulling. The S_n, that enters into equation (5.153) may then be calculated by taking the space Fourrier component of equation (5.147) as dictated by equation (5.150):

$$S_n(t) = -\frac{2}{L}\frac{\wp^2}{\hbar}\frac{E_n^0}{\gamma_{ab}}\int_0^L \frac{U_n^2(z)}{1 + (\wp^2 E^2/\hbar^2\gamma_a\gamma_b)\,U_n^2(z)}\,dz \qquad (5.155)$$

At the onset of oscillations we may neglect the saturation factor in the denominator. The integration is then unity and replacing in equation (5.153), we obtain the start oscillation condition for the properly tuned resonator:

$$\boxed{\frac{1}{Q_n} = \frac{\wp^2 \mathcal{N}}{\hbar^2\varepsilon_0\gamma_{ab}}} \qquad (5.156)$$

For oscillation we see that like in the microwave maser we must have a resonator which has the highest Q possible. The other parameter partly under the control of the experimenter is $\mathcal{N}$ which is a measure of the population inversion; it is made large by choosing the proper atoms and buffer gas arrangement.

Although the analysis given here does not study all details of the basic principles of lasers, it is, however, very illustrative and gives the essential points of the theory necessary for understanding the operation of such devices.

Appendix A

*Table of angular momentum coefficients**

$$U_{M_J}^J = \sum_{mm'} C(jj'mm', JM)\, u_m^j v_{m'}^{j'}$$

is obtained reading down one column. We can also use the table in reverse order where

$$u_m^j v_{m'}^{j'} = \sum_{JM} (jj'mm'JM)\, U_M^J$$

		U_1^1	U_0^1	U_0^0	U_{-1}^1
$u_{1/2}^{1/2}$	$v_{1/2}^{1/2}$	1			
$u_{1/2}^{1/2}$	$v_{-1/2}^{1/2}$		$\sqrt{\dfrac{1}{2}}$	$\sqrt{\dfrac{1}{2}}$	
$u_{-1/2}^{1/2}$	$v_{1/2}^{1/2}$		$\sqrt{\dfrac{1}{2}}$	$-\sqrt{\dfrac{1}{2}}$	
$u_{-1/2}^{1/2}$	$v_{-1/2}^{1/2}$				1

		$U_{3/2}^{3/2}$	$U_{1/2}^{3/2}$ $U_{1/2}^{1/2}$	$U_{-1/2}^{3/2}$ $U_{-1/2}^{1/2}$	$U_{-3/2}^{3/2}$
u_1^1	$v_{1/2}^{1/2}$	1			
u_1^1	$v_{-1/2}^{1/2}$		$\sqrt{\dfrac{1}{3}}$ $\quad$ $\sqrt{\dfrac{2}{3}}$		
u_0^1	$v_{1/2}^{1/2}$		$\sqrt{\dfrac{2}{3}}$ $\quad$ $-\sqrt{\dfrac{1}{3}}$		
u_0^1	$v_{-1/2}^{1/2}$			$\sqrt{\dfrac{2}{3}}$ $\quad$ $\sqrt{\dfrac{1}{3}}$	
u_{-1}^1	$v_{1/2}^{1/2}$			$\sqrt{\dfrac{1}{3}}$ $\quad$ $-\sqrt{\dfrac{2}{3}}$	
u_{-1}^1	$v_{-1/2}^{1/2}$				1

---

* See for instance: V. Heine, *Group Theory in Quantum Mechanics*, Pergamon Press (1960).

		U_2^2	U_1^2	U_1^1	U_0^2	U_0^1	U_{-1}^2	U_{-1}^1	U_{-2}^2
$u_{3/2}^{3/2}$	$v_{1/2}^{1/2}$	1							
$u_{3/2}^{3/2}$	$v_{-1/2}^{1/2}$		$\sqrt{\dfrac{1}{4}}$	$\sqrt{\dfrac{3}{4}}$					
$u_{1/2}^{3/2}$	$v_{1/2}^{1/2}$		$\sqrt{\dfrac{3}{4}}$	$-\sqrt{\dfrac{1}{4}}$					
$u_{1/2}^{3/2}$	$v_{-1/2}^{1/2}$				$\sqrt{\dfrac{1}{2}}$	$\sqrt{\dfrac{1}{2}}$			
$u_{-1/2}^{3/2}$	$v_{1/2}^{1/2}$				$\sqrt{\dfrac{1}{2}}$	$-\sqrt{\dfrac{1}{2}}$			
$u_{-1/2}^{3/2}$	$v_{-1/2}^{1/2}$						$\sqrt{\dfrac{3}{4}}$	$\sqrt{\dfrac{1}{4}}$	
$u_{-3/2}^{3/2}$	$v_{1/2}^{1/2}$						$\sqrt{\dfrac{1}{4}}$	$-\sqrt{\dfrac{3}{4}}$	
$u_{-3/2}^{3/2}$	$v_{-1/2}^{1/2}$								1

Appendix B

DESCRIPTION OF STATES FOR AN ENSEMBLE

Following the discussion of section 2.2, a classification may be made in the description of the states of systems and ensembles:*

u_n It is an eigenstate. The expectation value of an operator Q, in the quantum mechanical sense, for a system in such a state, is

$$\langle Q \rangle_u = \langle u_n | Q | u_n \rangle \tag{B.1}$$

Ψ It is a state of a system made up of a linear combination of eigenstates. If all the information is known on the system, such that the state of the system can be represented by this function, the system is said to be in a pure state. The expectation value of the operator Q is then:

$$\langle Q \rangle_\psi = \langle \Psi | Q | \Psi \rangle \tag{B.2}$$

P_k and Ψ_k If an ensemble is made up of systems whose state Ψ is not known completely, we then say that we have an ensemble in a mixed state. If P_k is the probability of finding a system in the state Ψ_k, the average value of Q for the ensemble is

$$\overline{\overline{\langle Q \rangle}} = \sum_k P_k \langle \Psi_k | Q | \Psi_k \rangle \tag{B.3}$$

---

* For a more elaborate discussion the reader is refered to W. Louisell, *Radiation and Noise in Quantum Electronics*, Sec. 6.5, McGraw Hill, New York, (1964).

Appendix C

ALTERNATIVE DEFINITION OF ϱ

In a less formal method than the one used in chapter 2, one introduces the density matrix definition by calculating the average value of an operator Q for an ensemble containing a quantity n of systems in various pure states Ψ_k.

The expectation value for a system in one of the states is:

$$\langle Q \rangle_k = \langle \Psi_k | Q | \Psi_k \rangle \tag{C.1}$$

The average value for the ensemble is:

$$\overline{\langle Q \rangle} = \sum_k P_k \langle \Psi_k | Q | \Psi_k \rangle \tag{C.2}$$

where P_k is the probability of finding a system in the pure state Ψ_k. Since:

$$\Psi_k = \sum_n a_{kn} u_n \tag{C.3}$$

we have:

$$\overline{\langle Q \rangle} = \sum_k P_k \langle \sum_l a_{kl} u_i | Q | \sum_n a_{kn} u_n \rangle \tag{C.4}$$

$$= \sum_{ln} \left(\sum_k P_k a_{kl}^* a_{kn} \right) \langle u_l | Q | u_n \rangle \tag{C.5}$$

We define:

$$\varrho_{nl} = \sum_k P_k a_{kl}^* a_{kn} = \overline{a_l^* a_n} \tag{C.6}$$

We finally obtain as it should:

$$\overline{\langle Q \rangle} = Tr \varrho Q \tag{C.7}$$

Another definition of the density matrix may also be formulated from equation 2.22 of section 2.

We have:

$$\varrho | u_m \rangle = \sum_n \varrho_{nm} | u_n \rangle \tag{C.8}$$

Multiply from the left by $\langle u_m |$ and sum over m.

$$\sum_m \varrho | u_m \rangle \langle u_m | = \sum_{nm} \varrho_{nm} | u_n \rangle \langle u_m | \tag{C.9}$$

The term on the left hand side is ϱ multiplied by the identity operator:

$$\sum_m |u_m\rangle \langle u_m| = 1 \qquad\qquad \text{(C.10)}$$

This last relation is proved by calculating the expectation value of the operator:

$$\langle \Psi| \left(\sum_m |u_m\rangle \langle u_m|\right) |\Psi\rangle = \langle \sum_l a_l u_l | \left(\sum_m |u_m\rangle \langle u_m|\right)$$

$$|\sum_k a_k u_k\rangle \qquad\qquad \text{(C.11)}$$

$$= \sum_l a_l^* a_l = 1 \qquad\qquad \text{(C.12)}$$

which proves relation C.10.

Using the definition of ϱ_{nm} given by equation (C.6) we finally obtain

$$\varrho = \sum_k P_k |\Psi_k\rangle \langle \Psi_k| \qquad\qquad \text{(C.13)}$$

defining ϱ as the ensemble average of the operator $|\Psi_k\rangle \langle \Psi_k|$.

Bibliography

1 DENSITY MATRIX

Books

C. P. Slichter, *Principles of Magnetic resonance*, New York, Harper and Row, 1963.

A. A. Vuylsteke, *Elements of maser theory*, Princeton, New Jersey, D. Van Nostrand Company Inc., (1960), Chapter 3, p. 100.

A. Abragam, *Principles of nuclear magnetism*, Oxford at the Clarendon Press, (1961).

R. C. Tolman, *The principles of statistical mechanics*, Oxford University Press, (1938).

Articles

U. Fano, *Rev. Mod. Phys.* **29**, 74 (1957).

A. G. Redfield, *I. B. M. J. Research Develop.*, **1–19**, 1957.

2 MAGNETIC RESONANCE (BASIC ARTICLES)

H. C. Torrey, "Transient nutation in nuclear magnetic resonance", *Phys. Rev.* **76**, 8 (1949).

E. L. Hahn, "Spin echoes", *Phyc. Rev.* **80**, 580–594 (1950).

H. Y. Carr, E. M. Purcell, "Effects of diffusion on free precession in nuclear magnetic resonance experiments", *Phys. Rev.* **94** 630 (1954).

S. Bloom, "Molecular ringing", *J. Appl. Phys.* **27**, 785 (1956).

F. Bloch, "Nuclear induction", *Phys. Rev.* **70**, 460 (1946).

N. Bloembergen, E. M. Purcell and R. V. Pound, "Relaxation effects in nuclear magnetic resonance experiments", *Phys. Rev.* **73**, 679 (1948).

E. M. Purcell, H. C. Torrey and R. V. Pound, "Resonance absorption by nuclear magnetic moments in a solid", *Phys. Rev.* **69**, 37 (1946).

3 SPIN EXCHANGE

Books

J. C. Slater, *Quantum theory of matter*, McGraw-Hill, (1951).

L. I. Shiff, *Quantum mechanics*, Third Edition, McGraw-Hill, (1968).

Basic articles

L. C. Balling and Al, "Frequency shifts in spin-exchange optical pumping experiments", *Phys. Rev.* **133**, 607 (1964).

P. L. Bender, "Effect of hydrogen-hydrogen exchange collision", *Phys. Rev.* **132**, 2154 (1963).

Hyatt Gibbs and Robert J. Hull, *Spin exchange cross sections for Rb 87–Rb*^{87} *and Rb 87–Cs 133 collisions*, *Phys. Rev 153, 132*, (1967).

H. W. Moos and R. H. Sands, "Study of spin-exchange collisions in vapors of Rb 85, Rb 87 and Cs 133 by paramagnetic resonance", *Phys. Rev.* **135**, A 597 (1964).

S. M. Jarrett, "Spin exchange cross section for Rb 85–Rb 87 collisions", *Phys. Rev.* **133**, A 111 (1964).

P. L. Bender, "Interpretation of frequency shifts due to electron exchange collisions", *Phy. Rev.* **134**, A 1174 (1964).

T. E. Stark, "An experimental determination of the spin exchange cross section of K 39 and Cs 133", *Thesis*, University of Michigan, (1966).

E. M. Purcell and G. B. Field, *Astrophysics Journal*, **124**, 542 (1956).

J. P. Wittke, "A redetermination of the hyperfine frequency of atomic hydrogen", *Thesis* (1955).

J. P. Wittke and R. H. Dicke, *Phys. Rev.* **103**, 620 (1956).

Francoise Grossetête, "Relaxation par collision d'échange de spins électroniques d'une vapeur alcaline orientée par pompage optique", *These*, Ecole Normale Supérieure, Université de Paris, (1967).

4   OPTICAL PUMPING

Books

R. Bernheim, *Optical pumping*, New York, W. A. Benjamin, (1965).

C. Cohen-Tannoudji and A. Kastler, *Optical pumping*, Progress in Optics, Vol. V edited by E. Wolf, North Holland Publishing Co., Amsterdam (1966).

Articles

A. Kastler, "Quelques suggestions concernant la production …", *J. Phys. & Radium* **11**, 255 (1950).

A. Kastler, "Optical methods of atomic orientation and of magnetic resonance", *J. Opt. Soc. Am.* **47**, 460 (1957).

W. B. Hawkins, "Orientation alignment of sodium atoms by means of polarized resonance radiation", *Phys. Rev.* **98**, 478 (1955).

J. P. Barrat and C. Cohen-Tannoudji, "Etude du Pompage Optique dans le formalisme de la matrice densité", *J. Phys. & Rad.* **22**, 329–448 (1961).

5   MASERS AND LASERS

Books

J. R. Singer, *Masers*, New York, John Wiley & Sons Inc. (1959).

A. A. Vuylsteke, *Elements of Maser Theory*, Princeton, D. van Nostrans Co. (1960).

Basic articles

J. P. Gordon, H. J. Zeiger, C. H. Townes, *Phys. Rev.* **95**, 282 (1954).

K. Shimoda, T. C. Wang, C. H. Townes, *Phys. Rev.* **102**, 1308 (1956).

D. Kleppner et al., "Hydrogen maser principles and techniques", *Phys. Rev.* **138**, 972 (1965).

D. Kleppner et al., "Theory of hydrogen maser", *Phys. Rev.* **126**, 603 (1962).

P. Davidovits, R. Novick, "The optically pumped rubidium maser", *Proc. of IEEE* Special issue on frequency stability, Vol. **54**, 155 (1966).

J. Vanier, "Relaxation in rubidium 87 and the rubidium maser", *Phys. Rev.* **168**, 129 (1968).

B. A. Lengyel, "Evolution of masers and lasers", *AM. J. of Physics* **34**, 903 (1966).

J. P. Wittke, "Molecular amplification and generation of microwaves", *Proc. of IRE*, p. 291 (1957).

W. E. Lamb jr., "Theory of an Optical Maser", *Phys. Rev.* **134**, 6A, 1429 (1964).

Index